Singing Cowboys and
Musical Mountaineers

D1571007

Bill C. Malone

Singing Cowboys and

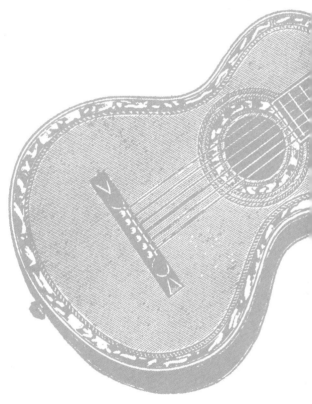

Mercer University
Lamar Memorial Lectures No. 34

Musical Mountaineers

Southern Culture
and the Roots
of Country Music

The University of Georgia Press
Athens and London

Designed by Erin Kirk
Set in 10 on 14 Goudy Oldstyle
by Tseng Information Systems, Inc.
Printed and bound by Braun-Brumfield, Inc.

The paper in this book meets the guidelines for
permanence and durability of the Committee on
Production Guidelines for Book Longevity of the
Council on Library Resources.

Printed in the United States of America

97 96 95 94 93   c   5 4 3 2 1

98 97 96 95 94   P   5 4 3 2 1

Library of Congress Cataloging in Publication Data

Malone, Bill C.
    Singing cowboys and musical mountaineers : southern
culture and the roots of country music / Bill C. Malone.
        p.   cm — (Mercer University Lamar memorial
    lectures ; v. 34)
    Includes bibliographical references and index.
    ISBN 0–8203–1483–8 (alk. paper)
    ISBN 0–8203–1679–2 (pbk.: alk. paper)
        1. Folk music—Southern States—History and criticism.
    I. Title. II. Series.
    ML3551.M26 1993
    781.62′13075—dc20   92-12430

British Library Cataloging in Publication Data available

Contents

Foreword

The appearance of Professor Bill C. Malone on the campus of Mercer University in the fall of 1990 was cause for celebration in more ways than one. Not only did the large audiences attending the thirty-fourth annual Lamar Memorial Lectures hear the results of excellent scholarship, they also heard beautifully performed country music. With Bill on guitar and his wife Bobbie on mandolin, the Malones illustrated the lectures by playing and singing not only secular favorites but traditional hymns as well. On one occasion Professor Malone provided what was undoubtedly a new experience to many in the audience by lining-out the old standard "Amazing Grace." The lectures that the music illustrated, presented here in expanded form, trace the protean origins of what came to be called country music, demonstrate the ways in which social preconceptions shape the course of that music's development, and unearth the reality that lies under the romance of southern plain-folk music.

From the path-breaking *Country Music, USA* through the present volume, Bill C. Malone, more than any other scholar, has established the musical expression of the South's plain folk as a subject worthy of serious study. Those members of the Mercer community and those townsfolk of Macon—a city justly proud of its own musical heritage—who were fortunate enough to hear his lectures are deeply grateful to him. His achievement at Mercer and in this volume amply fulfills the wishes of Eugenia Dorothy Blount Lamar, the founder of this series, who called for lectures "of the very highest type of scholarship which will aid in the permanent preservation of the values of southern culture."

Wayne Mixon
for the
Lamar Memorial Lectures Committee

Preface

      The invitation to present the thirty-fourth an-
nual Lamar Memorial Lectures was an honor which I will always
cherish. Not only was it immensely satisfying to participate in
a series that has featured so many distinguished scholars, but it
was also gratifying to receive a validation of my particular kind
of scholarship and of the subjects that I have chosen to empha-
size. It was fitting, too, that Macon should be the site of my lectures. Although those innovative sons of Macon—Phil Walden,
Little Richard Penniman, and Otis Redding—produced styles of
music far different from those that I emphasized, they nevertheless made their city one of the music capitals of the South while
also contributing immeasurably to the national popularization of
southern music.

      My wife, Bobbie, and I will always remember the gracious hospitality that we received from the Mercer University and Macon communities. Our short stay in the city was a pleasant interlude filled with stimulating conversation, delightful new friendships, and good music. We appreciate the special efforts made by Wayne and Frances Mixon and Henry and Patricia Warnock to make our visit comfortable and free of tension.

I would like to thank David Stricklin for compiling the index to this book. Most of all, my thanks go to Bobbie, who, as always, sustained me with her love, encouragement, intellectual stimulus, and mandolin playing.

Introduction

About thirty years ago, when I began research on *Country Music, USA*, I was preoccupied with the commercial history of a phenomenon that had evolved from southern regional roots into an industry with international implications. This was a rags-to-riches story that needed to be told.

Although the commercial history remained my central focus, other and larger questions emerged that could not be addressed immediately. I found, for example, that country music could not be understood adequately apart from its relationship to other musical forms that lay around it. That realization inspired an interest in all southern grassroots musical forms, which in turn resulted in *Southern Music/American Music*. I had always believed, and became more convinced as my research progressed, that country music's twentieth-century commercial development—from its first exploitation by radio and recording in the 1920s until its concentration in Nashville in our own time—was only one phase of a much older story that reached back to the beginning of the nation's history. I was similarly convinced that country music's development, from its obscure grassroots origins to its present-day commercial strength, was best understood as a phase in the history of the folk culture of the South. The growth, discovery, and eventual commercialization of southern rural musical forms, I believed, would tell us much about the values, self-perceptions, and historical evolution of the plain folk. I did not fully realize at the beginning of my research that the perceptions of the southern folk held by "outsiders" (i.e., northerners, foreign observers, middle- and upper-class southerners) were powerfully important in shaping both the definition and reception of the music identified with the folk.

As I moved farther back into the preradio sources of country music, the presumed British origins seemed increasingly less important as defining elements than I had once believed. The roots *were* British, in a very general and generic sense, but I could find no clear evidence that they derived from any explicit English, Irish, Scottish, or Welsh cultural soil. Romantic but enduringly popular terms like "Anglo-Saxon" and "Celtic" made even less sense as explanations for southern folk or country music styles. On the contrary, southern rural music seemed more and more to be a remarkable blending of ethnic, racial, religious, and commercial components with both Old World and American origins. "British" styles met and meshed with German, Spanish, French, Caribbean, Mexican, and African-derived forms. The result was the emergence of vigorous but localized musical expressions that retained distinguishing identities while also exhibiting the marks of their common crucible of development and interchange. As the multiethnic origins of southern music became apparent, the evidence of the rural South's unconscious eclecticism and cultural pluralism became more compelling. Above all, I found it increasingly difficult to link country music to any kind of "pure" ethnic, racial, or cultural heritage. The continued use in our own time of such terms as "Celtic," "mountain," or "western" to describe certain music styles reaffirmed for me the power of myth and symbolism in shaping the folk culture of the South and its music. It was obvious that southern music did not develop in a cultural vacuum, or in a context that drew sustenance only from its own indigenous resources; the music in its various manifestations largely responded to widely held notions about the South and of rural life, folk music, and the rural folk.

Except for an occasional reference to a fiddle contest or a sacred harp convention, southern white rural music received no apparent public attention until the World War I era. Until that time black musicians or their imitators—jubilee spiritual singers, blackface minstrels, ragtime piano players—dominated most conceptions of southern music. When the recognition of native white folk musicians finally came, in the years running roughly from 1910 to 1917, such interest was devoted almost exclusively to two immensely romantic groups, cowboy singers and Appalachian balladeers. The music of the majority of the southern plain folk, who lived in the interior South outside the southeastern mountains and far from the western plains, remained unnoticed and undocumented. This neglect, it seemed to me, was but the most recent manifestation of attitudes that dated back for well over a century of American life—*the failure by the larger society to take the plain folk seriously,* or the tendency to see them as culturally degenerate or, at best, as romantic children of nature. The real discovery of white plain folk music, and its introduction to the world at large, came in the 1920s when the radio and recording industries began their virtually simultaneous exploitations of ethnic and grassroots musical forms. By that time stereotypes of "poor whites," and conceptions of what "folk music" should be, had become so well fixed in the public mind and in the entertainment industry that it was well-nigh impossible for country musicians to perform without trying to meet someone else's expectations.

Country entertainers and their fans, however, were no more immune to the myths and stereotypes concerning southern rural life, both negative and positive, than was the larger American public. Although the musicians were essentially working-class people who were trying to survive, and build professional careers, in a society increasingly given over to middle-class values, they were more than willing to play the roles that the paying public expected of them. And, like most people in our consumer society, they were ambivalent about their origins and insecure about the new and highly impersonal world of the present. Uncertain about their real identities, musicians and public alike often sought escape in presumed representations of a mythical past. Since little or nothing in their backgrounds as workers or farmers provided the romance that mass entertainment craved, and since much in their cultures in fact repelled the sensitivities of a national audience, the musicians instead tried to link their music to accepted and appealing symbols. Hence the proliferation of musical mountaineers and singing cowboys.

The first two essays that follow attempt to suggest the breadth of sources on which early commercial country music drew, while the third explores some of the mythology that contributed to the shaping of the music once its development as an industry began. These discussions are not intended to be definitive, and I am under no illusion that they even ask all of the right questions. The provocative issues presented here form part of a much larger study of country music and the southern working class that I am preparing for the University of Illinois Press. These essays also should be considered as preliminary and partial explorations in the full-scale study of southern folk culture that many scholars, including some who are found in the footnotes of this book, are conducting.

I hope that students, from the widest possible range of academic disciplines, will join the quest to illuminate the lives of the plain folk who have too long been viewed through the veil of neglect and romance.

Chapter One

Southern Rural Music in the Nineteenth Century

In a sense, the music that is now described as "country" was called into existence in the early 1920s by those powerful urban forces of technology, radio and recording. During that decade a disparate assemblage of fiddlers, banjo players, string bands, balladeers, yodelers, gospel singers, and other "grassroots" performers for the first time began making phonograph recordings and radio broadcasts.[1] A cluster of local styles, some of which were very old and whose origins lay in the Old World, and others which had a relatively recent New World genesis, gained access to an audience that was potentially national, and even international, in scope. To the great surprise of entertainment industry executives, this music struck a responsive chord not only in the South, where most of the performers lived, but also throughout much of the rest of America. Although the music clearly projected an image that was redolent of the perceived simplicity and morality of rural America, no one immediately labeled it as "rural." Such descriptions as "old-time," "old familiar," and "hillbilly" appeared in record catalogues and radio brochures during the first two decades of the music's development, but, surprisingly, "country" did not gain favor as an identifying label until the mid 1940s. "Country music," in fact, had never existed as a concept in the previous history of the United States, nor in the prior British experience. Historically, the only descriptive label that had suggested a rural-based music—"country dance"—had won currency primarily in the late seventeenth century among upper-class Englishmen, and dance instructors who catered to them, to indicate steps and measures presumed to be of rural or peasant origins.[2] Rural-oriented entertainers, it is true, had long thrived in the United States, as was befitting of a nation that gloried in its virtuous yeoman beginnings. For example, at the end of the nineteenth century such performers as Denman Thompson and Cal Stewart built careers playing rube or hayseed characters, and the tent-repertory theaters were famous for their red-thatched country boy characters, generically known as "Toby."[3] The powerful impulse for rural nostalgia that accompanied the nation's transition to urban-industrialism also stimulated the American popular song industry. A plethora of songs referred frequently to the old rural home and its values, sometimes with condescending humor, but most often with affection or with regret at their disappearance.[4] Nevertheless, neither the rural stage characters nor the rustic songs really indicated the existence of a discrete, marketable entity known as rural entertainment. The humor and songs were representations of rural life created or adapted by professional urban entertainers. While this material influenced both the musical repertory and self-conception of country people, the entertainment industry was nevertheless slow to recognize the possibility that a vast market, composed of both city and country people, might exist for rural music. One also finds no real concept of southern music in American entertainment prior to the twentieth century. A mythical South, of course, had appeared often in American popular music. Beginning with the blackface minstrels, a torrent of songs swept across America describing a romantic South filled with exotic people and enchanting scenes. By 1900 "longing for dem good old times in Dixie" had become one of the staples of Tin Pan Alley.[5] Northern musicians and songwriters were among the principal architects of the Romantic South, and the southern-born musicians, black and white, who gradually attained prominence after the Civil War clung closely to the patterns established earlier by Stephen Foster and his white minstrel cohorts. The black entertainers who began touring the country in minstrel troupes after 1865, along with Nashville's Fisk Jubilee Singers who introduced spirituals to the world in 1871, whittled away at the northern dominance of American music, and with the emergence of Scott Joplin and the ragtime pianists in the 1890s a legitimate southern presence began to be felt in American music. Southern white musicians, on the other hand, were conspicuous by their absence from the professional music scene at the end of the nineteenth century. To an American audience conditioned by a long exposure to black-face minstrelsy, Stephen Foster melodies, plantation spirituals, and ragtime tunes, "southern music" was "black music."

The music of the white folk South remained terra incognita to most outsiders until the decade following 1910 when John Lomax and Cecil Sharp, with their respective collections of cowboy and Appalachian songs,[6] "discovered" and introduced to America a sampling of the ballads and folk songs of the southern white plain folk. The songs emphasized by Lomax and Sharp, as well as the enormous variety of styles not represented in their books, shared the fate of the people who had nourished and preserved the music and therefore remained largely unrecognized for generations. Southern folk culture and music had been alternately scorned, viewed with condescension, exploited for their humor, romanticized, or, most often, merely ignored. But whether noticed or not by the folklorists, academicians, or entertainment industry, music had indeed survived and thrived among the rural people of the South.

White rural music should be defined simply, and logically, as music and dance that white rural people accepted as their own. Rural southerners made their own music or inherited it from their forebears, but they also absorbed songs, dances, instrumental pieces, and performing styles from whatever source was available within the total southern context in which they lived. A good tune was a good tune, whether wafted on the breeze by a town brass band, a militia fife-and-drum duo, a circus fiddler, a street corner evangelist, a black gospel singer, a minstrel banjoist, a piano roll, a disc or cylinder recording, or any other source that disseminated music. Lawrence Levine has reminded us of the ultimate irrelevance of musical sources, and his conclusions about the making of slave music speak just as strongly to those who would understand the total musical world of the white plain folk: "It is not necessary for a people to originate or invent all or even most of the elements of their culture. It is necessary only that these components become their own, embedded in their traditions, expressive of their world view and life style."[7]

Southern white folk music possessed no single defining ingredient. Some listeners think they hear the sound of a Celtic bagpipe in the strains of a country fiddle; others think that the African admixture gave country music its spark and vitality and therefore made it intriguing; a few believe that the styles of blackface minstrelsy contributed much to country music's early character;

others are convinced that southern Protestantism gave the music
its basic style and tone; while still others are positive that its long
history of isolation in the southern backwoods gave rural music a
tangy flavor and distinctiveness that set it apart from other forms
of music.[8] All of these influences, and more, were present in the
music of the rural South, but none exclusively defined its essence.
Precise knowledge of the South's early rural music will never be
available to us. No sound recordings inform our understanding of
style, and the few written sources that exist describe little more
than the social context in which music was performed. Travel
accounts and local color literature, for example, sometimes provide tantalizing glimpses of country dances and backcountry revival meetings, but they tell us little about musical performance
style or about the ethnic identities of the participants. So little
is known, in fact, that the possibilities for romantic speculation
become almost endless, and observers generally have not hesi-
tated to make bold and sweeping judgments about the South, its
people, and their music. The white folk South, many have argued, was "Anglo-Saxon," a pure racial strain that preserved both
the speech and folkways of Elizabethan England. This vision of a
pristine culture has survived into the second half of the twentieth century, even among some plain folk southerners who simultaneously claim Anglo and Indian ancestry! The Anglo-Saxon
myth has died hard, but it now seems on the verge of being sup-
planted by the Celtic myth, the belief that southern character was
the product of people who came from the "Celtic Fringe" of Great
Britain (Northern England, lowland Scotland, Ulster, Wales, the
Hebrides, and Ireland). Southern white folk music, so the theory
goes, was essentially a cluster of Celtic survivals brought to the
South principally by Scotch-Irish immigrants and preserved in the
songs, dances, and instrumental music of the region. A passionate
love for music and dancing, argues Grady McWhiney, the princi-

pal theorist of southern Celticism, was a Celtic trait that clearly distinguished Southerners from the dour "Saxon" inhabitants of New England and the North.[9] No one can refute the general observation that most early white southern immigrants came from the British Isles, or even that a very large percentage of them came from what David Fischer calls the borderlands or what others have described as the Celtic Fringe. Nor can one successfully challenge the certainty that they brought, and transplanted in southern soil, a variety of folkways that included music. David Fischer, in his bold and controversial book *Albion's Seed*, describes a wide array of practices and traits such as speech and naming patterns, house types, religious behavior, and food customs in the southern backcountry that bear close resemblance to folkways practiced in the British borderlands. Except to reaffirm that these border folk did indeed enjoy music, Fischer makes only a few passing references to the subject.[10] His reticence was probably wise, because the comparative research necessary for bold judgments about the survival of British music in America simply has not been done. We do not know enough about music and dance on either side of the Atlantic during the first two centuries of immigration to the North American colonies. One suspects, admittedly on the basis of very limited evidence, that music and dance moved as freely in the British Isles as did the plain folk of that troubled realm. Carl Bridenbaugh's assessment of the migratory habits of rural Englishmen of the years from 1590 to 1640—the period of the first significant migration to the American colonies—would also ring true for many other people in the British Isles: "they were a peripatetic lot, shifting here, moving there, traveling along the roads in incredible numbers. Furthermore, they had been changing locations ever since serfdom began to disappear in the fifteenth century."[11] David Fischer suggests a similar restlessness and mobility in the mid eighteenth century among the border immigrants, whom he describes as a "mixed people."[12] They were mixed, he argued, in social rank, religious preference, ancestry, and place of origin. Their music would have displayed a similar diversity of origin, reflecting not only the movement of people back and forth along the Scottish-English border, from Scotland to Ulster, and across northern England, but also the popularization of songs, ballads, and dances by itinerant professional musicians. People learned tunes and songs from broadside ballad vendors, tavern fiddlers, Punch and Judy puppet shows, and a host of other traveling musicians who disseminated musical items that already had traveled many miles before they ever reached the hands of their peddlers. In seventeenth- and eighteenth-century Britain, as in the American South, music observed few barriers. Consequently, the music that came to America reflected not the qualities of a specific ethnic group, but was instead the product of a centuries-old process of social and cultural interchange that involved many ethnic groups and social forces. Carl Bridenbaugh is correct in describing clannishness as "the most pronounced social trait" of the Scotch-Irish, Germans, and other Europeans who moved into the southern backcountry during the Colonial era. A pronounced cultural conservatism encouraged preservation of the "folkways" described by Fischer; folklorists, anthropologists, ethnomusicologists, and material culturists have built careers documenting the lingering evidence of these traits. But while each group "clung tenaciously to its cultural heritage,"[13] social and economic interchange, intermarriage, and the common experience of living in a newly developing land gradually whittled away at their exclusiveness. Both music and consciousness of ethnic distinctiveness eventually became subsumed in a larger folk culture that encompassed virtually all inhabitants of the South. At some indeterminate time, European ways became southern ways.

The process of acculturation for British immigrants began as soon as they reached America. The so-called Scotch-Irish, in any case, would not have found adjustment to an English-dominated society to have been too difficult since they had lived under English control for over a hundred years before coming to America. In western Pennsylvania—the principal seedbed of the southern backcountry—they found themselves neighbors to the also newly arrived Germans. The fiddle and fife, and a repertory of songs common to both instruments, became popular among Scotch-Irish and Germans. Samuel Bayard, a leading authority on folk fiddling in the United States, argues that while Scotch-Irish influence was far stronger, the Germans nevertheless made distinct and measurable contributions to the genre of fiddle music in Pennsylvania. Bayard, in fact, used the term "British-German" to describe what he called the "dominant and oldest imported tradition" in Pennsylvania. Don Yoder, in his superb study *Pennsylvania Spirituals*, makes a similar and instructive judgment about the folk religious tradition in the Keystone State: "Much of what we call Pennsylvania Dutch folk-culture is not a transplantation of Continental European practises onto Pennsylvania soil, but a new American production shaped by acculturation with the Scotch-Irish and English Quaker neighbors."[14] Like Bayard, Yoder admits that Scotch-Irish influence was dominant, and that such German revivalist groups as the United Brethren borrowed folk spirituals from their British neighbors.[15] It is clear, however, that Scotch-Irish musical expression in Pennsylvania was not a mere transplantation either; it absorbed influences, even if ever so slightly, from the groups around it. The process of acculturation was already well underway for both Scotch-Irish and Germans when they embarked on their journeys down through the Great Valley of Virginia and into the southern backcountry.

As the southern frontier pushed steadily toward the Southwest,

Scotch-Irishmen and Germans met and mingled with Scandina-
vians pushing in from the Delaware Bay, Englishmen coming in
from the Atlantic Coast, and with people whose origins represented perhaps a dozen other ethnic and racial elements from the
British Isles, the European Continent, and Africa. The folk culture that they created was neither racially nor ethnically homo-
geneous, but was instead the product of well over two centuries
of adaptation and interaction among the European and African
peoples who pushed the southern frontier from the Chesapeake
Bay to the woodlands of East Texas. The contributions made by
some groups were relatively few but nevertheless distinctive and
measurable. French dancing masters, for example, dispensed their
services most often among affluent planters and merchants, but
in so doing popularized a body of dance steps, instructions, and
songs that the plain white folk eventually claimed as their property. The famous square dance, once intimately identified with
the folk of frontier America, probably came to this country in
the cultural baggage of both British plain folk and French instructors; its surviving terminology, however, such as sashay, dos-a-
dos, promenade, allemande, provides enduring evidence of the
dance's origins in the French quadrilles and cotillions of the late
seventeenth century.[16]

Germans comprised a relatively small percentage of the total
southern population, with their chief concentration being in the
upper Piedmont region and in scattered areas such as South Central Texas, but they made decisive contributions to the musical
life of the South as teachers, symphonic musicians, instrument
makers and sellers, founders of music societies, brass band members, publishing house entrepreneurs and, of course, as folk fiddlers and gospel singers. These contributions touched the lives of
the plain folk in various ways, and in varying degrees of impact
(most of the Germans, of course, were plain folk themselves).

"Oom Pah" brass bands and polka bands could be heard in any community where Germans predominated. Sheet music and instruments bearing the imprimatur of German music stores circulated throughout the South. Although explicit documentation has not been found, Cajun French musicians in Louisiana are convinced that the accordion came to their culture from German sources (one recent authority refers to German-Jewish merchants).[17] On the other hand, German or "Bohemian" accordion bands did directly influence the styles of Mexican-American musicians in South Texas who developed a popular style now known as Conjunto.[18] While all of these influences were important, the most crucial and pervasive contribution made by German musicians to the building of the South's folk culture lay in the field of religious music. In about 1816 a German Mennonite named Jacob Funk established a small publishing house in the Shenandoah Valley of Virginia (in a community that later bore the appropriate name of Singer's Glen). There he published a modest little German-language songbook, *Choral Music*, which apparently enjoyed only a brief circulation. This initial and inauspicious publishing venture, however, marked the beginning of a shape-note music empire which, in the hands of his descendants after 1865, blanketed the South with songbooks and singing teachers.[19]

While descendants of white Europeans were fusing and reintegrating their inherited traits into a commonly shared folk culture, they also participated in a process of mutual exchange with their black neighbors. White solidarity, of course, in both a cultural and political sense, depended in large part on the presence of substantial numbers of black people in southern society. But black people were also indispensable elements of southern folk culture, and they made immeasurable contributions to its shaping and tone. The most expressive component of that culture, music, bears the unmistakable imprint of African-American style. Folklorist Norm Cohen, in fact, asserts that it is the African admixture that has set southern rural music apart from rural music elsewhere in the United States, and that it is also the ingredient that has made southern music appealing to people around the world.[20]

A realm of musical expression existed among antebellum blacks that was alien and often unknown to white people. Some songs, dances, and instruments clearly preserved the flavor and style of Africa. Antebellum blacks and whites, however, also played similar instruments, knew and performed many of the same songs and dances, or at least preserved a vocabulary of common reference and description. The term "frolic," for example, was typically used by both groups to describe a community dance, and the fiddle served as the predominant instrument at such affairs. Informants for the WPA Slave Narratives recalled a large body of fiddle tunes, hymns, minstrel pieces, parlor songs, and dances that also thrived in white tradition. String bands flourished in black communities long after the Civil War, and remnants of this tradition endured in certain parts of the South well after the burgeoning of ragtime and jazz.[21]

Despite the evidence of a shared body of songs and dances, it is difficult to find precise corroboration of antebellum musical interchange among poor whites and blacks. Antebellum newspapers, travel accounts, and other written sources make frequent references to slave fiddlers, but they are seldom described in a social context that includes white plain folk. Few yeoman farmers or poor whites received invitations to the plantation balls and soirees for which slave musicians usually played, even though they did occasionally attend the political barbecues, weddings, or other community social functions where the planters demonstrated their wealth and power. Plain white folk had frequent opportunities to hear slave musicians, but evidence of musical activity by humble whites, directed to or in the presence of slaves, is hard to come by. Although strongly discouraged by the planter class, social communion among poor whites and slaves had never been totally absent in the antebellum years. Active biracial interchange seems to have been the norm rather than the exception in the early colonial Chesapeake society, where white indentured servants and black slaves worked, worshiped, hunted, fished, drank, fought, played, and slept together.[22] There is no reason to think that they did not also share music, even if the proof of such exchange is only circumstantial. Such social intimacy diminished dramatically in the late seventeenth century as the percentage of slaves multiplied, as their propensity for independent community increased, and as the controls regulating their movement and behavior proliferated. No white person, however, rich or poor, would have been unaware of the musical skills of the blacks, and awed references to their singing, dancing, and instrument playing abound in the literature of the pre–Civil War period. Slave singers, for example, made themselves conspicuous at the great revivals of the early nineteenth century. Plain folk and slaves attended the famous Kentucky camp meetings of the early 1800s, and, although required to sit in separate sections, they also frequently attended the same church services during the antebellum era.[23] These quasi-integrated religious gatherings permitted a shared musical experience that no other setting could provide. Each group was exposed directly to a common body of songs, and to each other's performance style.

The Civil War affected the music of white plain folk in ways that have not yet been explored. In striking a deathblow to slavery, the war liberated both the slave and his music from the quarters. The "freedom" triggered by the war permitted a process that both changed the music of the blacks and made it increasingly available to the eyes and ears of the poor whites. To a degree never previously available during the restrictive days of slavery, poor whites during the postwar years became exposed to the music of black singers and musicians: in the guise of street singers; barrel-house, honky tonk, and brothel pianists; gospel and sanctified singers; medicine show performers; minstrel and vaudeville entertainers; and, of course, as workers on prison chain gangs, railroad construction lines, in coal mines, and other work projects. Ironically, plain whites came into their most intimate contact with black musicians at the moment when the music of black culture was in dramatic transition. Strong remnants of the older rural tradition of string band music endured among black entertainers, but, in the decades that followed emancipation, black styles increasingly reflected the rhythms and resonance of the city. Elements of this altered musical consciousness—in the forms of ragtime, blues, jazz, and gospel—dramatically reshaped the music of the southern white folk in the years that spanned the turn of the century.[24]

More immediately, the Civil War exposed white plain folk to a diversity of songs and musical styles much wider than those familiar in their home areas.[25] Men and boys from all over Dixie mingled on the battlefields, in the long marches and bivouacs, and in hospitals and churches, and came away from the encounters with new tunes and songs and probably with new ways of performing them. Fife-and-drum units and regimental brass bands strived to bolster morale and generate fighting spirit. Paperback, pocket-sized songsters and hymnals circulated by the thousands within the Confederate ranks, making available a body of songs that would also have been familiar to Yankee soldiers, but containing an increasing number of items contributed by native poets and songwriters.[26] Although few Confederate soldiers would have needed the encouragement, evangelists passed out hymnals and led the singing of religious songs. Minstrel troupes, quartets, or other professional musicians, such as the Irish-born Harry

Macarthy of "Bonnie Blue Flag" fame, sometimes provided entertainment, and occasionally a compassionate family or civic group
would invite a few soldiers to a private "musicale," hymn ses-
sion, or dance. More often, Johnny Reb made his own music—
privately whistling, humming, or singing a few fragments of a
hymn or love song that recalled the old folks or a sweetheart back
home, or joining some of his musical campmates in a jam ses-
sion or impromptu dance. Most of the musicians were amateurs,
but one finds occasional examples of professional or semiprofes-
sional experience among the soldiers. Professor F. W. N. Crouch,
the writer of "Kathleen Mavourneen" and other genteel popular
songs, sang around the campfires to his comrades in the Richmond Howitzers. Capt. Frank Cunningham, "best known by his
wonderful gift of song," sang often to his comrades-in-arms, and
by the time he died in Richmond in 1911 he was regionally famous
for his performances before Baptist conventions and for "thousands of funerals."[27] The professional standing or civilian musical experience of Sgt. William H. "Bill" Dean is unclear, but
the performances that he and his "troupe" gave each night for
fellow soldiers in the First Virginia Infantry were richly appreciated. Dean's group made "the woods resound" with such minstrel
tunes as "Nelly Was a Lady," "Come to De Ol' Gum Tree," and
"Sound, Sound De Banjo."[28] Pvt. Sam Sweeney, on the other
hand, did have minstrel experience, and was the brother of the
celebrated five-string banjoist, Joel Walker Sweeney, from Appo-
mattox County, Virginia. Prior to his death from smallpox in
1865, Sam had been Gen. J. E. B. Stuart's personal musician, and
was the leader of a string band that included the general's multi-
talented black body servant, Bob, who played fiddle, bones, and
guitar.[29]

String band music of the type dispensed by Sweeney and his
colleagues was not unknown to most rural Southerners before the

Civil War, but it is rarely described in antebellum sources. The banjo-fiddle combination, for example, had long been a staple of blackface minstrelsy, but its existence among prewar rural Southerners has been rarely documented. It seems reasonable to assume that minstrelsy was a prime conduit through which the banjo eventually reached rural Southerners, but it also seems likely that the instrument, and styles of playing it, became available to a large number of Southerners during the Civil War through the occasional concerts made by professional minstrels and through the informal jam sessions of soldiers. A wide variety of instruments, ranging from the fife to the accordion and guitar, showed up in the cargo of Confederate soldiers. The fiddle, of course, was the instrument most often heard in camp, just as it was throughout the rural South. No Confederate soldier would have been unfamiliar with the instrument, but when he went back home, he might have carried a larger repertory of tunes and perhaps a new lick or two learned from fellow soldiers.

The Confederate veteran returned to a home that urgently cried for music. Surrounded by bitter reminders of war's defeat, and by a grinding poverty that lasted into the next century, Southerners turned to those cultural and spiritual resources that had always provided nurturance and succor in times of distress. Some sought the security of religion. Most reaffirmed the values of family and home, even though, for many plain folk, that home was humble and often abandoned in the economically unsettling days that followed the war. The world of the rural Southerner had changed in dramatic and traumatic ways, but basic, sustaining elements of his culture endured. Music remained a vital presence in his life—lightening his work, dispelling his loneliness, enriching his worship, entertaining his friends and family, releasing his pent-up emotions, and accompanying him in his successive moves across the southern frontier and, eventually, into economic spheres far different from his ancestors'.

The precise delineations of the rural Southerner's precommercial musical environment can never be fully re-created. We can partially reconstruct the arenas of public performance represented by the fiddle and hymnbook because contemporary observers sometimes commented about dances where the fiddle held sway or camp meetings and other religious services where sacred music filled the air. But the larger and more intimate universe of private or domestic music will continue to defy complete understanding. Prior to the awakening of interest in Appalachian and cowboy balladry in the early years of the twentieth century, the vocal music of the rural South, both secular and religious, remained almost completely ignored and undocumented. Except for an occasional reference to the group singing heard in the camp meetings, or perhaps a stray comment about vocal music in Confederate musical camps, travelers and other observers of the nineteenth-century South had surprisingly little to say about noninstrumental songs and even less to say about vocal style. Consequently, most of what we know, or think we know, about precommercial singing comes from analyses made of folk singers' repertories and styles in the twentieth century. And most of these discussions have concentrated on singers from the Appalachian Mountains. It has been widely and perhaps rightly assumed that some of the singers heard on commercial hillbilly recordings in the 1920s, and those who were documented on field recordings in the 1930s, had preserved songs and styles that dated from a much earlier era. Alan Lomax correctly maintains that musical style is "one of the most conservative of culture traits" because style, like language, is acquired early in one's life and is intimately intertwined with personality formation. Music therefore functions as "an important link between an individual and his culture," [30] and its style of performance changes very slowly. But while it is reasonable to assume that a culturally conservative people will preserve traditional modes of performance, we should be mindful also that, as Lawrence Levine reminds us, "culture is not a fixed condition but a process: the product of interaction between the past and present." [31] Conservative Southerners inherited a large body of musical material from their European and African forebears, but this rich corpus was augmented by repeated infusions of new songs and alternative styles of performance in the many decades that followed the American Revolution. Few communities in the rural South remained isolated from the encroachments of the market economy, and even the most remote corners of the southern Appalachians had been touched by the forces of industrial change at the end of the nineteenth century. Southern country boys also went off to war in 1775, 1812, 1846, 1861, 1898, and 1917. Neither musical style nor repertory remained unchanged under the assault of such compelling forces.

Cecil Sharp and other collectors demonstrated during the first two decades of the twentieth century that a surprising number and variety of British songs survived in the South, and that they in fact lay at the core of the Southern rural repertory. Although most collectors placed Child ballads at the top of their musical hierarchy, there is no reason to believe that rural Southerners valued these imported or inherited songs any more highly than those of native origin. Deeply cherished songs like "Barbara Allen" and "Lass of Roch Royal," or variants of them, were nevertheless subsumed in a larger body of music that was also loved and whose sources often defy precise determination. We cannot even be certain about how, and by whom, the British material was brought to the South. Ballads and folk songs did come with the British immigrants, but the individual contributions made by the English,

Scotch-Irish, Welsh, or other groups within the British spectrum cannot be measured. Nor can we assume that these songs came to America in the exclusive possession of poor people; the venerable ballads, after all, have been collected often in the homes of middle- and upper-class families.[32] Indeed, some very popular ballads, such as "Mary of the Wild Moor," "Daddy, Don't Go to the Mines," and "Rose Connelly" ("Down in the Willow Garden"), and fiddle tunes such as "Ricketts Hornpipe" and "Fisher's Hornpipe," came to America, not with the "plain people," but with professional British entertainers who toured the United States in the decades following the American Revolution.

The primacy of music in folk communities is well established, but the varying roles played by men and women in its preservation is a topic that awaits further exploration. It has long been assumed that although men and women performed different types of music, women were the chief conservators of culture, and therefore of music, in the white folk South. Alan Lomax, for example, said that "for some considerable time, and especially in America, the ballads have been women's songs, attached to the household and the fireside. The men, left to themselves, sang humorous or bawdy songs which satirized love, or composed songs about work or deeds of violence."[33] Domestic singing, that which was centered in the home and directed at family or friends—as opposed to the aggressive, masculine arts of fiddling or banjo playing—was presumed to be the province of women. One of the most eloquent descriptions of the separate spheres occupied by rural men and women—"a rift that is never closed even by the daily interdependence of a poor man's partnership with his wife"—is that of Emma B. Miles in her classic volume *The Spirit of the Mountains* (1905). Referring to her neighbors and kin in the Tennessee hills, Miles said that the man "conquers his chosen bit of wilderness, and heartily begets and rules his tribe, fighting and praying alike fearlessly and exultantly. Let the women's part be to preserve tradition. His are the adventures of which future ballads will be sung. . . . The woman belongs to the race, to the old people. He is a part of the young nation. His first songs are yodels. Then he learns dance tunes, and songs of hunting and fighting and drinking, and couplets of terse, quaint fun. It is over the loom and the knitting that old ballads are dreamily, endlessly crooned." [34] The list of outstanding southern male ballad singers is long—one thinks, for example, of such people as Dillard Chandler, Doug Wallin, Horton Barker, Jason Ritchie, Buell Kazee—but the observations made by Miles and Lomax have the ring of truth about them. Women have made powerful contributions to the art of balladry, and, like Jane Gentry of Hot Springs, North Carolina, who in 1916 provided Cecil Sharp with his single-largest batch of traditional songs (sixty-four), [35] they have been invaluable informants to those interested in preserving such material. Because of the intimacy of their relationship, mothers inevitably influenced the songs that were learned and remembered by their children, the style and inflection of their singing, and the morality and aesthetic sense that may have shaped their future musical choices. Some songs were sung consciously to children to amuse, divert, or comfort them. Children learned other songs unconsciously through repeated exposures to favorite ballads and hymns, as mother privately voiced her longings, her joy, or her loneliness and pain. The old songs were loved by men and women alike, but for women they may have assumed a somewhat more special meaning. Through the associations and memories they evoked the songs became links to a cherished past, and were therefore worthy of preserving as one would a photograph, a lock of hair, a quilt, or some other sentiment-adorned memento. Some of the songs may also have summoned up alternative, and even darker, visions of present reality for many women. Alan Lomax has argued that some pioneer and backwoods women may have embraced the old songs, not merely as expressions of emotional release, but because they "represented the deepest emotional preoccupations of women who lived within the patriarchal family system." [36] The "old lonesome songs," with their tales of unrequited and unfaithful love and of lovers who died for love, were widely popular among both men and women, but they may have found a special resonance with many women who saw their own lives mirrored in the lyrics. The "bloody ballads" may have played similar roles in permitting the vicarious projection of covert but aggressive feelings. Most women may not have harbored murderous passions toward insensitive spouses or lovers, or toward ungrateful children, but songs like "Little Mattie Groves" and "Lord Thomas and Fair Eleanor," with their tales of sexual intrigue and murder, provided catharsis for many women whose lives were blighted by deprivation and pain and loveless marriages.

Most vocal music circulated and endured in the rural South in the manner described above, as an informal and often unconscious exchange among family and friends. The basic process of song dissemination was oral, as evidenced by the wide and pervasive existence of song variants and fragments. The ubiquity of a ballad like "Barbara Allen," known to Americans in a profusion of tunes and texts, reminds us that the ear and memory are imperfect instruments. Singers typically tried hard to preserve songs as they first heard them, but lyrics were forgotten, words were misunderstood, phrases and melodic structures were unconsciously altered, and "improvements" were consciously made to songs that did not quite fit either the individual's or the community's musical aesthetics. The oral process, however, was a necessity to the folk; they did not make a fetish of it. Nor did they scorn other methods or sources for learning and preserving songs, whether from a printed songster or newspaper songsheet or, eventually, from a radio broadcast or phonograph recording. Favorite songs were hand-copied on single sheets of paper, usually called "song ballets," or in school tablets. Song texts were clipped from magazines and newspapers and then pasted to the pages of an old book. Printed song collections entered the homes of the plain folk in a variety of guises: in pamphlet-size folios advertising concerns such as the Cable Piano Company or Hamlin Wizard Oil, in religious tunebooks or gospel hymnals, in pocketbook songsters or garlands, or as sheet music.

We actually know much more about the songs, and about the ways in which they moved into the rural repertory, than we do about their styles of performance. In the absence of sound recordings, "style" necessarily remains a poorly understood and sketchily researched phenomenon. Except for religious congregational singing, such as that heard at sacred harp conventions, one finds little discussion of vocal performance in the pre-twentieth-century South. Given the universality of singing in the white rural South, it is remarkable that travelers and other observers of the region had so little to say about the art. Our speculations about solo vocalization in previous centuries depend almost completely on surviving nineteenth-century religious tunebooks, which generally included sections on the "rudiments" of singing (instructions about proper methods of singing), or on observations made in this century of rural singers, with most of them coming from the Appalachian or Ozark South. Scholars read the descriptions made by early collectors, such as those of Emma Bell Miles in her pioneering essay of 1904, "Some Real American Music,"[37] or the commentary made in 1916–1918 by Cecil Sharp, or they listen to the performances of older singers on commercial hillbilly recordings from the 1920s or to the music collected on field recordings in the 1930s and assume, perhaps rightly, that the styles and songs heard there are survivals of a much earlier period, and that they have remained basically unchanged. Alan Lomax, one of the few scholars who has been bold enough to enter this forbidding area of musical inquiry, is probably correct in arguing that "culture" and "style" are linked—i.e., that vocal performance is strongly shaped by such factors as childhood rearing, community standards, and religious values. His further assertions that southern white folk vocal style was a consequence of a religiously repressive and sexually inhibited culture is certainly suggestive, and perhaps correct, but it is a judgment that begs for more extended research.[38] Deductions drawn from limited samplings—mostly from twentieth-century mountain singers—may tell us little about the people of the larger South and about those who had close contacts with black singers. One should also recall that those "inhibited" people of whom Lomax speaks, with their tight, constricted throats, are also the people who are alleged to have frightened Yankees with their wild rebel yells. Until persuasive evidence is made available, we should probably discard the thesis of a pervasive white folk style, and should posit instead the probability of many "styles" that, though similar enough to invite comfortable fusion, reflect the differing communities and subcultures from which they came.

While religion does not hold the single key to an understanding of southern rural musical style, its pervasive influence nevertheless cannot be ignored. As Howard Odum perceptively noted, "much of the religion of the South was expressed through song," and this music "not only brought forth the sweep of social heritage and individual memories but touched deep the chords of old moralities and loyalties."[39] The domain of religious music encompassed the lives of virtually all rural Southerners, and one finds nowhere a stronger linkage of tradition, world view, and life-style. Within this realm, where rural Southerners received their strongest encouragement to sing, even the most repressed and burdened person found a means of individual expression and a source of community bonding. Religion was not simply a source of music; it was also a powerful shaper of the mood, tone, and performance style of all the music of the South, spiritual and secular.

The dissenting religious sects who populated the South—the Baptists and Methodists who came in from the Atlantic Seaboard, and the Presbyterians and German Pietist groups who came down the Great Valley of Virginia from Pennsylvania—brought traditions of music that wedded secular tunes to religious lyrics. Most would have easily agreed with the assertion, attributed to a musically tolerant English Anglican minister, Rowland Hill, that there was "no reason why the Devil should have all the good tunes!" The English composers Isaac Watts and Charles Wesley supplied Methodism with a large body of songs that eventually made their way into the repertories of the southern evangelical groups. Songs like these, and the "folk spirituals" of anonymous origin, fueled the great revivals that swept across the Virginia countryside in the 1740s, and again across the Kentucky frontier and the upper South sixty years later.[40] In the emotional atmosphere of the Kentucky camp meetings, where large crowds found encouragement to sing, but where few books and little formal instruction were available, religious songs were further democratized by the use of simple, singable melodies, repetitive phrases, and choruses and refrains. Songs of southern camp-meeting origin generally circulated orally and anonymously—except for a few known to have been composed by men such as John Adam Granade and Caleb Jarvis Taylor—but, as early as 1805, the texts of some of this material began to appear in camp-meeting songsters; their circulation in the North, and their appearance in Northern-compiled tunebooks, such as John Wyeth's immensely influential *Repository of Sacred Music, Part Second* (1813), constitutes, perhaps, the first documented example of southern influence on American music.[41]

The birthplace, and subsequent seedbed, of southern religious rural music appears to have been in southwestern Virginia, or what Richard Hulan describes as the corridor between Lancaster, Pennsylvania and Abingdon, Virginia, among the Scotch-Irish Presbyterians, German Protestants, and Methodists who fortuitously shared and combined their gifts of song. Hymnbooks were being published in the Shenandoah Valley as early as 1816 and 1817, when Jacob Funk's *Choral Music* (totally in German) and Ananias Davisson's *Kentucky Harmony* appeared. Camp-meeting songs, authentic and otherwise, appeared in these and similar books alongside the older folk spirituals, the formal hymns of Watts and Wesley, and newly composed songs from the American experience.[42] As early as 1816, then, the categories of songs that comprised the southern rural religious repertory had largely fallen into place. That repertory was not substantially altered until the emergence of gospel music after the Civil War.

Throughout the nineteenth century, and in fact during much of the twentieth, most southern hymnals were characterized by shape-note notation—a simplified system invented in New England in which musical syllables were indicated by assigned shapes rather than by their positions on the staff. Singing schoolteachers took this system to virtually every community in the rural South, while southern-based publishers provided them with songbooks such as *The Sacred Harp, Christian Harmony,* and *The Southern Harmony,* which are still venerated by many rural Southerners or their urban relatives.

The shape-note writers and publishers contributed mightily to the crafting of southern rural music throughout the nineteenth century. They introduced and popularized a body of songs that entered the repertories of Southerners everywhere, and, through the ubiquitous ten-day singing schools, they taught several generations of Southerners how to read and sing music. Although hardy and indefatigable singing teachers had already taken the

shape-note method as far west as Texas by the beginning of the
Civil War, this system of musical proselytizing did not become a
systematized and elaborately organized business until after 1865
when two of Jacob Funk's descendants, Aldine S. Kieffer and
William H. Ruebush, built their shape-note empire at Dayton,
Virginia. Kieffer and Ruebush published songbooks; established a
"normal school" that, under the direction of Benjamin Unseld,
trained hundreds of potential teachers; sent those instructors to
communities all over the South; and linked religious singers everywhere through their widely circulated magazine, *Musical Million*.
Farther south, in Dalton, Georgia, Anthony J. Showalter, the
composer of "Leaning On the Everlasting Arms" and another de-
scendant of Jacob Funk, opened still another music house whose
representatives blanketed the lower South with songs, singing
schools, songbooks, and instruction manuals.[43]

   After the Civil War shape-note methodology became linked to
a kindred phenomenon, gospel music. Although the term "gospel" was not used in print to describe a body of music until 1874
when Philip P. Bliss's *Gospel Songs* appeared, the songs found
there had already begun to circulate, North and South, in the
tracts and hymnals distributed to soldiers during the Civil War,
as elements of the YMCA and Sunday school movements, and as
part of the city revivals led by evangelists like Dwight Moody and
Ira Sankey of Chicago. Written predominantly by such northern
writers as George F. Root, Will Thompson, Philip Bliss, and the
blind poetess Fanny Crosby, the songs soon became powerful vehicles of sectional reconciliation. Allied closely in style, mood,
and often in theme with the popular music of the day, items
like "The Ninety and Nine," "Softly and Tenderly," and "Beautiful Isle of Somewhere" moved into the permanent possession
of the southern people and can still be found in many southern
denominational hymnbooks.[44]

While heavily indebted to northern writers and publishers, Southerners nevertheless produced a large body of indigenous gospel material, some written especially for denominational hymnbooks, and some for the shape-note publishing houses that proliferated in the South.[45] This music shared the fate of all mass-produced popular culture—much was ephemeral and of questionable quality—but many of these songs endured as beloved and integral expressions of the collective southern experience. On the other hand, whether of northern or southern origin, the gospel songs found few friends among the "better music" fraternity, and the mainline denominations eventually purged most of the songs from their official hymnbooks. Passionate battles concerning the choice of songs found in the hymnbooks, or over the replacement of congregational singing by choirs with professionally trained choirmasters, almost tore some churches apart. Many old-time Christians complained bitterly about the abandonment of the more "democratic" or participatory musical styles and interpreted the purging as part of a more pernicious trend of increasing coldness and formalism within Protestantism, a falling away from the original faith. Gradually, the older varieties of shape-note singing, the gospel hymns, and the congregational mode of performance retreated to the rural and small-town churches, or found refuge in the working-class churches of the cities. Such denominations as the Church of Christ, the Primitive Baptists, and the Old Regular Baptists of Appalachia retained much of the spirit, as well as the songs, of the early southern folk church. Many southern Christians, however, found a new and satisfying fusion of old-fashioned fervor and updated techniques in the worship practices of the Holiness and Pentecostal sects, which began to flourish at the end of the nineteenth century. With their spirited, camp-meeting-style songs, congregational singing, ardent receptivity to all varieties of musical instruments and performance styles, and emotional fervor, these congregations did much to restore a folk consciousness to southern Protestantism. Most of the pioneers of the grassroots Holiness campaigns are unknown today, but they made themselves dramatically visible in their own day by the power of their singing. One contemporary observer of a Holiness convention in North Carolina in 1897 noted that "the people sang in the Spirit, and such singing as we had never heard before. The very air was laden with the spirit of these songs; and as we returned home from the meeting that night, we could hear the different crowds going their respective roads singing." Sarah E. Parham spoke similarly of the singing done by Pentecostals in the Houston area during the summer of 1905: "O, the heavenly singing in the various languages, under divine inspiration, was something one could never forget."[46] Much like the camp meeting congregations of the early nineteenth century, black and white Christians interacted often in the Holiness and Pentecostal revivals of the late 1890s, despite an increasingly rigid climate of legal segregation. Much of the history of this phase of Holiness or Pentecostal revivalism is irrecoverable, but the story of an African-American couple, Brother and Sister George Goings, is probably not unique. With Nashville as their home base, the Goings preached and sang the Holiness message throughout Tennessee and Kentucky in the last years of the nineteenth century, and by 1901 they had taken their sermons, and famous songs like "There's A Little Black Train A Coming," to the streets of California.[47] Whether black or white, Pentecostal evangelists, such as George Goings, armed with guitar and Bible, accompanied perhaps by a mandolin-strumming or tambourine-shaking wife, and preaching on street corners, under brush arbors, in tents, or in storefront churches, took their places alongside the shape-note teachers and gospel quartets as major agents in the fashioning of the southern gospel music repertory. Songs from that repertory, learned in Sunday school and church, at revivals and protracted meetings, in singing schools and conventions (the sites of the famous "all-day-singings-with-dinner on the grounds"), and on the streets of any southern town, shaped the consciousness of a broad spectrum of Southerners, assuring a common frame of reference and shared heritage for people from varied walks of life. Powerfully inspired and permanently affected by their religious experiences, some southern Christians drew definite distinctions between "sacred" and "sinful" music, and refused to perform the latter for fear of eternal punishment. The old ballads and love songs, and the lively fiddle, sometimes fell victim to the abandonment of "worldly pleasures" that often followed the experience of personal conversion.

Despite the attraction of religion and the accompanying guilt concerning secular music, most Southerners had a hard time keeping their feet from tapping when the rhythms of the dance began. An observer of late-eighteenth-century social mores in Virginia was referring to upper-class Southerners when he said "they will dance or die."[48] But the observation would have been equally true of the plain folk. The piety and restraint engendered by the revivals of the nineteenth century actually did little to inhibit the universal passion for dance found among rural Southerners. Restraint was certainly not a defining characteristic of that "other side" of rural southern culture, the frolic, where dancers gave vent to a freedom with their feet that they did not always permit with their voices. "Frolic," a term of British origin, was widely used in the South by both blacks and whites to describe almost any kind of social or community affair centered around dancing. The frolic generally accompanied community labor, such as corn shucking, house raising, or quilting; but weddings, Fourth of July or Christmas parties, political barbecues, or almost any kind of excuse might prompt such a celebration. Frolics of course might differ in size and social intent, but their general characteristics actually changed very little in the several decades that followed A. B. Longstreet's description of a country dance on the Georgia frontier in 1835. Continuing a tradition that would have been familiar to rural Georgians and other Southerners as late as 1935, the furniture was first removed from a room in the small country house, whereupon the family and their invited guests danced most of the night to the accompaniment of a black fiddler, and then topped off the evening with a sumptuous feast at midnight.

Longstreet's account tells us a great deal about the social contexts surrounding the country dances. The recollection of the black fiddler reminds us of the biracial influence that did so much to mold rural music. The Longstreet-described dance was held in the rough cabin of a local county officeholder, suggesting that such music cut across and, indeed, often blurred class lines. Longstreet—a man of property, education, and breeding—recalls the "good old republican reels" of his youth, and waxes nostalgic about their disappearance.[49]

While his discussion recaptures the spirit and zest of the backwoods frolic, neither Longstreet nor any other contemporary observer really recounts the precise details of nineteenth-century rural music. Observers described the social settings where the music held sway, and the names of musical instruments, songs, and dances heard and seen there, but they indicated little about the style of musical performance and dance. Not only was music of merely incidental interest to most of the pre-twentieth-century witnesses, very few possessed musical training, or the skills necessary to judge, understand, or communicate the nature of "folk" or noncultivated musical performances. Although some of the genteel observers, for example, were certainly exposed to formal dancing instructions in their youth, only a few would have known enough about the art to be able to describe the rough-hewn dance steps they saw. What they saw at the country dances, after all, tended to be not merely adaptations or variations of European dances, but fusions of dances borrowed from several sources, or nothing more than the makeshift improvisations of the dancers themselves. Observers did sometimes mention dance steps such as "jigs," "double shuffles," "breakdowns," and "pigeon wings," and general references to cotillions, reels, or quadrilles were often made.[50] Typically, however, descriptions went no further than that of the famous traveler and usually acute social observer Frederick Law Olmsted, who referred to "feats of prolonged dancing, or stamping upon the gallery," which he observed near the Sabine River in Louisiana.[51] The English traveler Charles Lanman likewise whets but does not satisfy our curiosity when he mentions "a series of fantastic dances" that he saw at Black Mountain, North Carolina, in the early 1850s; the German Frederick Gerstaecker is not much more enlightening when he speaks of "the extraordinary movements" of the dances he saw in backwoods Arkansas at a Fourth of July frolic.[52] But neither Olmsted, Lanman, nor Gerstaecker is as frustrating as Julian Ralph, who in the midst of an excellent and detailed account of his travels in the South some forty years later, says, "I wish there was room for descriptions of their dances!"[53]

Descriptive terms like "pigeon wing" or "buck-and-wing," along with references to certain tunes and songs, suggest that the music of professional blackface minstrelsy had become part of the repertoire of backwoods Southerners well before the Civil War. Gerstaecker, for example, while not using the term, nevertheless describes something very close to "patting juba" (the practice of rhythmically slapping the knees and chest while dancing), which he observed during one of his backwoods Arkansas sojourns. Rural dances, however, were probably marked more by improvisation than by the conscious imitation of professionals. A correspondent to the *Spirit of the Times* in 1843 revealingly described an East Tennessee rural dance: "The music sounds high, and the wild woods ring; the feet of the company fly thick and fast; reels, cotillions, and waltzes, are all so mingled and blended together that it is a dance without a name."[54]

A similar cloak of imprecision obscures the history of the musical king of the southern frontier, the fiddler. Fiddlers arrived early in the southern colonies—Earl Spielman credits John Utie's arrival in Virginia on the "Francis Bonaventure" in 1620 as the earliest example[55]—and they remained omnipresent in the South throughout the nineteenth century. However, fiddlers evoked ambivalent images that reflected the shadowy origins of their European past. They carried the taint of the "sturdy beggar" of Elizabethan England, and the even older image of the "Devil as a fiddler." Accounts of drunken or ne'er-do-well fiddlers appear frequently in eighteenth- and nineteenth-century sources, including ads for runaway indentured servants. Col. Alexander Walker, who had been a minor political figure in the early Arkansas territory, presented a relatively benign version of fiddlers when he said that God had created all things beautiful except whistling women, crowing hens, fiddlers, fire-dogs, and popcorn.[56] Many religious people, both black and white, took a much dimmer view, depicting the fiddler as a wastrel, or as a person who lured other people toward sin. Even in the twentieth century A. P. Carter, the pioneer white country musician, had to hide his love of the fiddle from his religious mother.[57]

The image of the fiddler as rogue or rambler is romantically appealing, but greatly exaggerated. Simultaneously prized and despised, the fiddler's talents often spread his name far and wide beyond his home community. Joseph C. Gould, recalling his youth and young adulthood in middle Tennessee during the Jacksonian era, declared that "the lyre of Apollo was not hailed with more delight in primitive Greece, than the advent of the first fiddler among the dwellers of the wilderness."[58] Skill at fiddling often won more than mere invitations to dances, or prizes at fiddle contests; as it generated good will among people, it also contributed to political and business success. The well-known tale of "the Arkansas Traveler" may be apochryphal, but it accurately suggests that music could be a powerful healer of personal and even social divisions. In some versions of the tale, the inhospitable rube and the lost city dweller remain separated by mutual suspicion until the latter demonstrates that he too can play the fiddle.[59]

We cannot be certain of the Arkansas Traveler's identity, but he appears to have been a man of some substance. His demonstrated ability on the fiddle reminds us that the art of fiddling in the nineteenth-century South was not confined to the poor. Poor whites, drovers, flatboatmen, yeomen, slaves, and free blacks did play fiddles, but so did planters, lawyers, judges, local political officials, governors, U.S. congressmen and senators, and even ministers of the gospel. We should resist the temptation to convert this evidence into a vision of Frank Owsley's harmonious and classless South,[60] but we should reject equally the idea of a region and society rigidly stratified and divided along impassable social lines. A common rural society defined the lives of virtually all Southerners, and a common folk culture encompassed the experiences of planters, plain whites, and blacks. Class stratification and racial bias did not prevent the mutual exchange of songs and dances, nor did a shared musical preference weaken the power of the ruling elites; if anything, it strengthened that power. Southerners on more than one occasion in their history have rewarded political candidates who demonstrated musical ability, or who expressed an affection, real or feigned, for the music of the plain folk. Tom Watson, the fiery Georgia Populist, and the Taylor Brothers (Bob and Alf) from Tennessee were merely the most famous examples of a large body of nineteenth-century politicians who exhibited a talent for old-time fiddling.[61] Although old-time fiddling could be used for political purposes, its primary function was social, and its most expressive arena was the frolic. We should therefore devote some attention to the kind and style of music that might have been heard there. Contemporary observers, in both the antebellum and postbellum periods, have provided us a listing of dances and fiddle tunes that suggest varied origins: Old World dance music, minstrel pieces and other "pop" songs, and American frontier dance tunes of mixed racial and ethnic origin. Later evidence, suggested by material found on early hillbilly recordings and in the reminiscences provided by older musicians, indicates that rural musicians adopted new songs and styles as they became available. Ragtime tunes, marches, waltzes, coon songs, and a variety of other material drawn from popular entertainment moved into the repertoires of the country fiddlers alongside the "rustic" tunes of earlier years. As the new century began, country fiddlers were generally prepared to play anything from "Soldier's Joy," "The Eighth of January," and "Flop-Eared Mule" to "*Sobre Las Olas*" (Over the Waves), "Under the Double Eagle," and "Dill Pickle Rag."[62]

Even though the names of songs played in the pre-twentieth-century South can be determined, early written sources tell us little about fiddle performance. Informants' use of such unenlightening terms as "sawing" and "scraping" to describe rural fiddle technique adds nothing to our understanding. A few lithographs and paintings from the nineteenth century provide minimal information about the way some fiddlers held their instruments, but the contemporary written and published records say almost nothing about tuning techniques, fingering, bowing, or the way the fiddle was held.[63] Early commercial recordings do provide some documentation of pre-twentieth-century styles. Some of the fiddlers heard on early commercial recordings, such as Fiddlin' John Carson, Am Stuart, Uncle Bunt Stephens, and Uncle Eck Dunford, were born well before the end of the nineteenth century.[64] Other fiddlers from the early commercial period undoubtedly learned much of their technique from relatives or friends who were born in the previous century and, in some cases, long before the Civil War. A series of tunes recorded as late as 1976 by the superb North Carolina fiddler Tommy Jarrell suggest the instructive possibilities of some modern recordings. Jarrell learned most of the songs heard on this album early in the twentieth century from older musicians, at least two of whom, Preston "Pet" McKinney and Zack Paine, were Confederate veterans. He introduces each song, such as McKinney's version of "Sail Away Ladies," with spoken commentary about its source and style, provides some recollections about the older musicians from whom the songs were learned, and then tries to play the tunes exactly as he had learned them.[65]

Despite the suggestiveness of these and similar modern recordings, we nevertheless should be very cautious about making bold and unequivocal judgments about the styles or ultimate origins of tunes that have precommercial histories. Some listeners think they hear the strains of bagpipes, or other "Celtic" instruments, when they listen to country fiddling today. One record album annotator, for example, responding to the music of early commercial fiddler Eck Robertson, surmised that *all* southern country fiddling may have stemmed from only a handful of Celtic styles.[66] Someone else, listening to Doc Roberts, Robertson's great fiddling contemporary from Kentucky, might presume that country fiddling came from black or vaudeville ragtime sources.[67] Still another listener might wonder how two presumably Celtic fiddlers, like Eck Robertson and Clayton McMichen, could sound so different from each other, and why Fiddlin' John Carson's style bore little resemblance to either of those two musicians. Southern fiddlers clearly did preserve "British" stylistic traits, but they modified them through a wide variety of experiences on the shifting American frontier: as they came in contact with fife players in eastern Pennsylvania, when they heard the music of traveling professional entertainers, or as they listened to the omnipresent black fiddlers of the rural South. We should not forget that individual fiddlers often introduced their own innovations, whether to satisfy a creative urge, to gain the upper hand in competition with each other or simply to delight their dancing customers, or merely to lighten the boredom of playing for long hours at a country dance. And when they heard a new and interesting tune, they adopted it, without worrying about its origins, though it might have come from a fife-and-drum band, a village brass band or circus orchestra, a minstrel string band, or a ragtime piano roll or phonograph recording.

The evolution of country fiddling, like that of gospel music in the South, reminds us that neither the music nor the culture in which it thrived was stable or static. The histories of country fiddling and gospel music vividly testify to the racial and ethnic diversity and social pluralism of the South. Southern rural music was built out of the cultural traditions of many interacting cultural groups, and in a context that, from the beginning of southern history, was always changing in conscious or unconscious ways. The southern plain folk, we are told, have always been marked by their mythic "sense of place," yet an opposing reality of movement and social dislocation has distinguished their history. They sing of an old home place, and a way of life, that have remained tangible only in memory or music. We are also told that rural Southerners through choice and geography were cut off from the outside world. Their presumed isolation, however, was never so complete as to prevent contact with other peoples and cultures, and they were never immune, nor necessarily opposed, to the economic interrelationships that have bound Americans to each other and to other people throughout the world. The first dramatic evidence of that economic and technological interrelationship came with the building of the railroads into many nooks and crannies of the rural South.[68] Continued signs of that contact came with the exploitation of the timber, coal, textile, and petroleum resources of the region. The rapid expansion of the market economy after the Civil War inevitably drew the humblest farmer into an intricate and international web of economic relationships.[69] Change, and linkage to the outside world, came at different rates, and at different times, to different groups of plain people throughout the rural South. Not even the supposedly well-insulated mountain South remained untouched by these economic transformations; indeed, the changes in the Appalachians were more immediate and more dramatic.[70] Everywhere these economic metamorphoses evoked frustration and bewilderment, and, in some cases, provoked bitter and violent resistance—as any student of Populism or Bloody Harlan, Kentucky, should know. After all, a familiar world was being dismantled. I cannot make a comfortable assessment of the total costs or gains that came from the confrontations between a tradition-oriented people and technology and industrialization. But neither am I prepared to say that the southern folk strongly resisted the machines that saved them time, reduced the labor and pain of life, and brought them closer to each other and to the varied cultures of the world, or that they resisted the powerful industrial innovations that delivered jobs or promised economic security.

Standing on the threshold of the twentieth century, the southern folk inhabited a world that, in many ways, was still very much like that of their grandparents. But it was a world that had been under siege since well before the Civil War. And it had only a few more decades of life.

Music had accompanied the successive transformations in the lives of the plain folk, and it accompanied them into the new century and, ultimately, into their new lives as wage laborers in towns and cities across the entire nation. Music contributed to their evolving self-definition as country people displaced from their rural moorings.

Only two short decades after the turn of the century, two new powerful forces of communication—radio and recording—permitted the scattered and localized forms of southern rural music to coalesce into a commercialized entity that eventually became known as country music. As radio broadcasts blanketed the nation's airwaves, and recordings penetrated into increasing numbers of homes, these commercialized vehicles of a shared regional culture provided security and escape for country folk in transition. Although residences and occupations changed, music endured, documenting the transformations that reshaped the lives of southern plain folk, and bequeathing to all of us the rich legacy of their cultural experience.

Chapter Two

Popular Culture and the Music of the South

At a conference on traditional music held in Chapel Hill, North Carolina, in April 1989, ballad singer Doug Wallin presented a short program of songs he had learned growing up in that citadel of old-time music, Madison County, North Carolina, where Cecil Sharp had found his richest repository of traditional ballads. After reverently announcing that he would perform a song he learned from his mother, Berzilla, Wallin cleared his throat, and after a pause, launched into "After the Ball," the monster pop hit from 1896 written by Charles K. Harris. The story and the lyrics were basically as Harris had written them, but the modal melody and the style of presentation were Wallin's. Some of the eminent folklorists in attendance sat in embarrassed or stunned silence. The incident nevertheless tells us much about the musical catholicity and tolerance of the folk.

Wallin is not atypical. His experiences with popular music, or with commercial music, have been shared by the folk for as long as such music has been available. The proof lies in the published folk song collections; the unpublished material found in college and university archives in the South (often collected from students or their parents); in the handwritten "ballets," song folios, and other published material found in plain folk homes; and in the recordings made since the 1920s by hillbilly and folk musicians for the commercial phonograph companies and the Library of Congress.[1] In these repositories one finds abundant examples of the folk's receptivity to music of popular origin. Given the clear and strong biases of the collectors, who usually hoped to find British-derived material or its American equivalent, it is a wonder that so many of the pop songs actually showed up in the published collections (one also wonders what and how much was left out of the collections). Referring to the "penny dreadfuls," his name for the folk songs of known popular origins, James Ward Lee noted that "folksong collectors do not like to get them, but most find that for every 'real' folksong they collect, they get six or eight 'dreadfuls.'" He further concluded that "one of the things highbrow collectors do not like to admit, but are forced to, is that their informants have almost no taste whatsoever."[2]

The scholars and musicians who became preoccupied with folk music at the turn of the twentieth century labored under the spell of the great Harvard academician, Francis James Child, who since the 1880s had collected surviving literary specimens of 305 British ballads.[3] The "Child ballads" were prized for their impersonality, dramatic import, and literary content, and were consequently deemed to be the "aristocrats" of ballad literature. The "broadside" ballads, on the other hand, were the known products of professional writers (usually described by the scholars as "hacks"), which were hawked on broadside sheets or in folios in towns and cities throughout Great Britain and Colonial America.[4] Child-oriented scholars tended to see the broadsides, and other songs of popular origin, as decidedly inferior to the more literary Child ballads. The folk, in contrast, made no such distinctions. The collectors who went "song catching" in the southern mountains in the early twentieth century did not go there in an open-minded search for whatever the folk possessed; they went instead in quest of living examples of the Child canon. Similarly, the collections made in American public schools after 1914, under the auspices of the U.S. Bureau of Education, were motivated explicitly by the desire to find Child ballads that were still being sung. Ecstatic that a few of these songs still survived, but convinced that their days were numbered, the collectors went about their tasks with a great sense of urgency. Howard Brockway, American composer and professor of composition at the Juilliard School of Music, later recalled his first song-collecting expedition in the Kentucky mountains in 1916: "The hunt for particular and rare old Elizabethan ballads was one which made us thrill oftentimes as the gold-seeker must thrill when he finds proof of the presence of the precious metal. . . . It seemed sometimes to me as though I were groping and feeling my way with the singer's mind through the generations back into the England of the seventeenth century from which his forefathers had journeyed forth into the fabulous New World!"[5] Whether "high-art" musician looking for concert material, literary scholar, or mountain settlement teacher, early collectors generally assumed that the British ballads and folk songs were the products of a rural "Anglo-Saxon" peasantry that was rapidly succumbing to the forces of industrial "progress" and racial dilution. Anything that smacked of the music hall, the popular stage, or Tin Pan Alley was interpreted by the collectors as unpleasant evidence that the old ballad art and the folk culture that nourished it were disappearing from the American scene.

Long before Howard Brockway and other song catchers made their trips to the southern hills, and well before Francis James Child put his first thoughts on paper, the songs, dances, and performance styles of popular culture had moved among and had been embraced by the common folk. A rather circular or reciprocal process of folk-popular musical interchange began long before the settlement of America. Professional entertainers, who were sometimes products of folk communities, often absorbed music or dances from folk sources, and then recirculated that material in presumably altered form among both cultivated and noncultivated audiences. The folk, on the other hand, learned songs or dances from professional musicians that over time and through repeated transmission were transformed into folk pieces of anonymous origin and composition. Except in a few cases, we do not know the identities of the itinerant musicians and ballad makers of the Middle Ages, nor do we know the sources of the music they performed. The pipers, fiddlers, jig dancers, or ballad vendors who entertained on street corners and village greens or at the rural fairs or other social or community functions, or who displayed their talents in taverns and alehouses, were as "commercial" as their societies would permit them to be. It is now impossible, and irrelevant, to assess properly their varying degrees of "folkness" or "professionalism."

Nor is it possible to identify or precisely define the music of those who performed with the traveling shows—the circuses, animal acts, Punch and Judy puppet shows, equestrian shows—and who disseminated music among the folk. It is very easy to dismiss them, along with the publishers and writers of the broadside ballads, as no more than crass opportunists who foisted their cheaply made music upon the gullible folk. But it makes no sense to exclude these musicians arbitrarily from the category of "folk." Of one fact we can be certain: the British folk who came to America

brought a mass of anonymous musical material that had been filtered through commercial and popular sources before it reached
their possession. Songs, dances, and performance styles often assumed wondrous and unexpected forms once they entered the
consciousness of the folk. The hornpipe, for example, began its
career as an instrument used to accompany rural dances. Eventually, a solo step dance known as the hornpipe, performed to the
accompaniment of either the pipe or the fiddle, became popular
throughout the British Isles. The hornpipe remained a folk dance
among rural people, but by the early eighteenth century it had
also become a showpiece for professional entertainers of varying
descriptions. The dance may have come to America in something
like its original folk form, but it was circulated most widely in this
country in styles perfected by trained dancers, like John Bill Ricketts and John Durang, who traveled with professional troupes.
Rural Southerners seem not to have preserved the dances popularized by these entertainers, but they embraced the tunes that
accompanied them. In the southern musical lexicon, a hornpipe
became nothing more than a fiddle tune.[6]

The southern plain folk exhibited a catholic receptivity to
musical forms and styles comparable to that of their British ancestors. The South remained throughout the nineteenth century,
and much of the twentieth, a pervasively rural society marked by
bad roads, widely separated communities, a relatively high percentage of illiteracy, and primitive methods of communication.
Nevertheless, its people were never so isolated as to be immune
to the currents of popular culture. The folk singer Jean Ritchie,
in her beautiful autobiography, *Singing Family of the Cumberlands*,
provides us with an instructive corrective to the myth of isolation.
In about 1905, her father, Balis Ritchie, and his brother, Isaac,
walked eighty miles from the freight office in Jackson, Kentucky
to bring home to their families in remote Perry County a brand-

new talking machine. During the return trip, which consumed several days, they delighted the folks with whom they stayed by playing cylinder records on the machine that "could talk and sing plime blank like a natural man!"[7]

Long before talking machines and radios infiltrated the nation's backcountry, pop music was already accompanying the traveling shows that journeyed all over rural America in the nineteenth century. The pattern was in fact set by the end of the eighteenth century when puppet shows, circuses, animal acts, medicine shows, equestrian shows, and, of course, formal dramatic and musical concert troupes traveled from town to town along the Atlantic Seaboard.[8] Most of the humble dancers, fiddlers, and other musicians who frequently traveled with such shows are undocumented and unremembered. Only someone like John Bill Ricketts, who was already famous in England before he came to America with his circus in 1792, is recorded in the standard studies of early theater. This great equestrian performer delighted audiences with his remarkable physical dexterity and timing— among other marvels of agility, he danced hornpipes on the back of a horse galloping around an arena. Country fiddlers still play a song known as "Ricketts' Hornpipe." Ricketts's famous American student and associate, John Durang, who in the 1780s became this country's first great professional dancer, also inspired an enduring fiddle tune, "Durang's Hornpipe." Composed in 1785 by Wilhelm Hoffmeister as a concert piece for Durang, the tune began the life that eventually led it into the repertories of country fiddlers all over America.[9]

The imported tradition of traveling entertainment endured in the young American nation where it was often intermeshed with the world of commerce. The medicine show, for example, whose ancestry dates from at least the Middle Ages, was a familiar presence in eighteenth- and nineteenth-century America (at least a thousand of these shows were documented in 1900). Traveling by flatboat and horse and wagon, medicine shows used music and comedy to sell their cargoes of magic elixir.[10] The patent medicines were consumed or discarded, but the melodies lingered on. Rev. Mason Locke Weems was not known as a medicine show spieler, but he did employ music to sell products. Best known as the inventor of the George Washington cherry tree story, Weems was also a peddler of books and moral tracts who traveled extensively by horse and wagon in the upper seaboard South in the early 1800s. Weems played lively fiddle tunes to attract country and small town folk to his sales pitches.[11] Nineteenth-century circuses, like all troupes of itinerant entertainers, welcomed the chance to travel through Dixie during the hard winter months. Musicians such as Dan Emmett who later made careers in blackface minstrelsy or other forms of show business first served apprenticeships with circuses like Spalding and Rogers. Although music was an indispensable ingredient of circus success, the shows differed greatly in the kind of performances they could afford. Some could hire only a fiddler; others used gaily costumed brass bands to announce their presence or to accompany their acts; and, of course, others used the infectious sounds of the calliope. Probably the most influential musical feature of the nineteenth-century circus, however, was the singing clown. Some clowns, like Dan Rice, became famous for singing the pop hits of the day, both silly and sentimental, and cheap editions of "clown songsters" were widely circulated among circus audiences.[12]

Like the other touring show business aggregations with which they competed, circuses differed greatly in the kind of pomp and splendor they could display. Few of the nineteenth-century traveling shows, however, were as lavishly outfitted and promoted as the showboats that carried theater and variety entertainment down the major rivers of Middle America. The showboat era of American entertainment began in 1831 when William Chapman took his elaborately decorated steamboat, "The Floating Palace," down the Ohio River for a season of theatrical productions. Before their day in American history was completed, Chapman and his competitors dispensed their brand of entertainment not only at ports from Pittsburgh to New Orleans, but also at tributary river towns far off the beaten track.[13]

Theatrical groups (or thespians, as they were often described) played major roles in the dissemination of popular music in the South. Presenting a diverse and rugged fare that ranged from Shakespeare to melodrama to variety entertainment, these men and women had to be prepared to perform as singers, dancers, musicians, and actors. Music was often part of the theatrical productions themselves, but songs and dances were also commonly interspersed between acts as sets and costumes were being changed. One can only be impressed by the hardihood and missionary zeal of such early theatrical people as Daniel Drake, Sol Smith, and Noah Ludlow, who traveled thousands of miles with their troupes on flatboats down the Ohio and Mississippi rivers, and by horse and pack into interior areas not easily reached by boat. In 1822 Noah Ludlow introduced in New Orleans the "pop hit" of that year, and a song which would soon play a vital role in Andrew Jackson's campaign for the presidency—"Hunters of Kentucky"—to a wildly enthusiastic crowd of visiting flatboatmen and local residents. These groups, though, took their brand of culture to places much smaller than New Orleans. Sometime in 1833 Sol Smith's group presented an evening of Shakespeare in the dining room of a hotel in tiny Tazewell, Alabama. If Shakespeare could reach a small town like that, pop music certainly could too.[14]

Of all the traveling shows known to nineteenth-century Americans none had a more pervasive impact than blackface minstrelsy.

The phenomenon's overall history need not concern us here, except to say that it was a form of variety entertainment performed for most of its history by white men in blackface.[15] Students of the form generally concentrate on the years from roughly 1840 down to the end of the century. Minstrelsy's influence, however, could still be detected up to the middle decades of the twentieth century, and its influence on the music of the South has been enduring and profound. Abundant opportunities existed throughout much of the nineteenth century for professional musicians to absorb the sounds and styles of the folk South while also introducing their own music into the culture. And well before the formal founding of the first minstrel troupe in 1843—the Virginia Minstrels—individual blackface musicians, performing usually as members of circus acts, were already touring through the South. Minstrelsy remained an active presence in the South until at least World War I, and blackface comedians in fact thrived in the region's entertainment until the early 1950s—a cork-faced duo known as Jamup and Honey headlined the Grand Ole Opry's number-one tent show in the year prior to the landmark Supreme Court decision, *Brown* v. *Board of Education,* which outlawed racial segregation in the public schools.[16]

Minstrel-derived humor did indeed endure in country music, and can still be heard on most any "Hee Haw" television segment in our own time. Minstrel influence, however, went far beyond mere stage costuming or plantation-style humor. Minstrelsy also introduced or popularized an abundance of songs, dances, instruments, and instrumental and vocal styles that moved into the repertories of southern rural folk. The relationship between minstrel music and folk music, of course, is about as difficult a problem as we are likely to encounter. The minstrels were itinerant song-and-dance men who borrowed potentially commercial music wherever they traveled, in both town and country, and from every available ethnic source. Some songs and styles undoubtedly came from "plantation Negroes" or other "folk" sources, but other musical ideas, such as those that informed the work of Stephen Collins Foster, came from the reciprocally transmitted body of popular music available to both European and American musicians.[17] As Hans Nathan has argued, the popularity of the term "minstrel" itself, as well as the standard employment of four entertainers in the early minstrel ensembles, may have been inspired by the Tyrolese Family Rainer, a popular Alpine troupe that came to the United States in 1838. Nathan notes further that while the tunes used by the early minstrel groups "seemed original at the time, most of them turned out to be variants of stage and folk music of Great Britain."[18] The minstrels of course were also inventive entertainers who reworked older material, while also creating new musical ideas. Some minstrel songs and styles, then, were simply recycled to the folk who had originally "created" them, while others were newly introduced. In either case, it is difficult to document the explicit transmission of style or song from minstrel performer to folk performer, because minstrel material sometimes went through a variety of formats before it finally reached the "people"—through medicine shows, vaudeville, burlesque, tent-repertoire shows, chautauqua, itinerant entertainers and, eventually, phonograph recordings and radio broadcasts.[19]

Minstrel fiddlers and banjo players abounded. Backed by an array of rhythm instruments such as bones, tambourine, or triangle, the fiddle and banjo constituted the closest approximation of a "string band" that most rural Southerners had ever seen, and the two remained the most common coupling of instruments in the rural South up to the 1920s. The prevalence of minstrel fiddlers and banjoists, and their exposure to southern audiences over a period of several decades, suggests a strong influence. But while minstrel tunes, such as "Old Dan Tucker," "Turkey in the

Straw," and "Arkansas Traveler," have appeared frequently in the repertoires of southern folk and country musicians, the imprint of minstrel performance *style* has been much harder to document. One finds virtually no contemporary description of minstrel fiddling, or fiddle instruction books from the nineteenth century. Hans Nathan, in his otherwise excellent discussion of the life and career of Dan Emmett, is frankly making a bold and unsupported leap in the dark when he says that "Emmett performed like a real country fiddler; he held his instrument in front of his chest and drew his bow across the strings as if it were an unwieldy pole." Nor does he provide any documentation for his assertions that Emmett played with a "squeaky, carelessly tuned fiddle" or that his style featured "occasional variants including dotted notes and syncopations, and with open strings as drones, as is still the custom in the backwoods." [20] Even if these descriptions of early minstrel fiddle style are correct, we are still left with the question of who influenced whom. Was the early minstrel style merely an approximation of rural fiddling? To what degree was it inspired by the playing of black fiddlers? And, conversely and most important for our purposes, what was the extent of minstrel influence upon the style and repertory of southern country fiddlers?

The five-string banjo, on the other hand, elicited extensive contemporary commentary, enough in fact to make its history both bewildering and intriguing. Although the banjo eventually played a dramatic role in the history of commercial country music and was at the center of the bluegrass style's evolution after World War II, the instrument's popularity among rural musicians lagged far behind that of the fiddle throughout most of the nineteenth century. Antebellum references to the banjo's presence among rural whites are rare, and only during the Civil War, when Confederate soldiers played string band music on bivouac, does one find suggestions that the instrument enjoyed extensive usage in the South. Songs mentioned in the Civil War recollections indicate minstrel influence, as does the testimony given much later by the pioneer country musician Uncle Dave Macon. Macon's recollections of having learned banjo techniques in about 1885 from Joel Davidson, a minstrel who stayed at his parents' boardinghouse in Nashville, constitutes one of the few direct testimonies that is available of such influence; his recorded repertory, however, including songs like "Rock About My Saro Jane," provides dramatic audio evidence.[21]

It is easy to understand how the banjo, and the minstrel style, could have reached Dave Macon in Nashville, or other potential musicians in those places easily reached by touring professional entertainers. The banjo also gained currency and became increasingly respectable in other formats available principally to city people in the decades after the Civil War. Polk Miller, for example, a Richmond pharmacist, became regionally famous in the 1890s and early years of the twentieth century with his programs of southern and Confederate songs presented periodically to civic groups and Confederate reunions. Miller played the banjo and appeared with a group of black musicians known as the Old Southland Quartette.[22] By the turn of the century banjo, mandolin, and guitar clubs had become the rage among middle-class youth on college campuses and in towns and cities throughout the South, and a variety of playing styles—some of them borrowed from guitar techniques—were made widely available in instruction books and on the recordings of such popular urban musicians as Fred Van Eps and Vess Ossman.[23]

Despite the popularity the instrument exhibited in the urban South at the end of the nineteenth century, the banjo nevertheless became most strongly identified as a southern mountain instrument. How did an instrument of black origin become identified with a region where few blacks lived and where access to the outside world was limited? The answers to the questions of how the banjo reached the mountains, and how mountain styles evolved, would do much to clarify the larger process of folk and popular cultural interchange. Robert Winans feels that the available evidence suggests white minstrel influence in the years following the 1880s when steamboats, following such Ohio River tributaries as the Big Sandy, took professional troupes far back into the hills. He also argues that surviving banjo instruction books from the 1850s reveal that such presumed "mountain" banjo styles as "frailing" and "clawhammer" were adaptations of antebellum minstrel techniques. William Tallmadge, on the other hand, argues for direct black influence on the mountaineers, and maintains that the banjo took root in the Appalachians with blacks who lived there before the Civil War, and was made additionally popular by blacks who moved to the mountains after the 1870s to work in the coal mines or on the railroads.[24]

While minstrelsy's impact on southern musicians was profound and enduring, its most important legacy lay in the songs that it bequeathed to America. No phenomenon, in fact, did more to generate a songwriting industry in the United States. A host of songwriters, including Stephen Foster, contributed to the "Ethiopian business" in order to survive or prosper in the music trade. Like Foster, the writers may have aspired to genteel acceptance, but they also needed commercial sustenance—and that meant writing songs for the minstrel troupes. The minstrels are popularly identified with nonsense songs like "Old Zip Coon," or faithful darkey laments like "Old Black Joe," but no songs or performance styles were excluded from their repertories. Ever alert to the tastes and changing fashions of the American public, minstrelsy became a vehicle for the dissemination of the whole range of American popular music, including sentimental and mother songs.[25]

Most of the minstrel songs were ephemeral, but a large number outlived the entertainment form that gave them birth. "Old Zip Coon" (best known as "Turkey in the Straw"), "Buffalo Gals," "Listen to the Mockingbird," "Old Dan Tucker," "Yellow Rose of Texas," "Jordan Am a Hard Road to Travel," "Away Down on the Old Plantation," and, of course, "Dixie," were but a few of the minstrel-born songs that eventually assumed folk status. Many became staples of hillbilly or country music.

Minstrelsy's role in funneling songs to the southern folk was but a phase in a much larger and older process of pop and folk music interchange. Prior to the concentration of song publishing in New York City in the 1890s, in the district around 28th Street known as Tin Pan Alley,[26] the publishing business was decentralized in a variety of cities including New Orleans, Chicago, Cincinnati, Boston, and Milwaukee. Although minstrelsy provided a powerful vehicle for the national distribution of pop music, sheet music became the chief source of income for publishers and songwriters. Generally accompanied by colorfully illustrated title sheets, these songs provided Americans with a cheap source of both popular art and music. When displayed on the stand of the parlor organ or piano, sheet music also conveyed fashion, respectability, and achievement of bourgeois status.[27]

Like most of the pop culture of the nineteenth century, the illustrated song sheets, and the pianos on which they rested, were aimed principally at the literate and increasingly affluent middle-class audience of America's northern cities. The themes of the songs, however, most often dealt with commonplace events and people. As Nicholas Tawa has noted, the lovers described in such songs tended to be "drawn from the middle or nonurban lower class. Rarely do they represent the rich or well-born. Usually they dwell in 'cots' or 'cottages' on mountains, in valleys, or by the sea."[28] Regardless of the origins or authorship of the songs, a great many of them moved into the hinterlands, North and

South, and their durability remained evident well into the following century's Jazz Age. The popularity of such songs in the
South is clearly revealed, as we have seen, by their presence in
the standard folk song collections, where their original identities
are seldom recognized or noted, on the nostalgia pages of early-
twentieth-century magazines and newspapers where favorite old
songs were requested, and, of course, in the repertories of hillbilly
musicians who kept them alive in the decades after 1920.

All varieties of nineteenth-century pop music made their way
into the rural South, but songs of sadness, nostalgia, and sentimentality seemed to find the greatest reception there. The death
and devastation wrought by the Civil War surely contributed to an
overall mood of sadness and insecurity that lingered as long as the
sufferings and separations of the war were remembered. The pervasive poverty that clung to the region for many decades following
the war, combined with the unyielding disintegration of the old
economic order, inspired nostalgia for and romanticization of the
past and uncertainty for the future. With the disappearance of the
open range and the burgeoning of tenantry in the closing decades
of the nineteenth century, the horizons of the plain folk narrowed
dramatically. The Holiness Revival of the post–1870s era brought
reassurance to many poor people; music, as always, offered additional comfort and security. It is no wonder that songs recalling
an earlier vanished society, or extolling the virtues of hearth,
home, and country church, or remembering the Sainted Mother
who had stood at the center of one's moral universe, should find
great favor among rural Southerners in the closing decades of the
century.

Some of the songs that filtered into southern popular consciousness came from the pens of writers well known to students of American popular music: Septimus Winner ("Whispering
Hope," "Listen to the Mockingbird," "What is Home Without a

Mother"); Henry Clay Work ("The Ship That Never Returned," "Come Home Father," "Grandfather's Clock"); James K. Bland ("Carry Me Back to Old Virginia," "Oh Dem Golden Slippers"); Charles K. Harris ("After the Ball," "Hello Central Give Me Heaven," "Mid the Green Fields of Virginia"); Gussie Davis ("Baggage Coach Ahead," "The Fatal Wedding," "Maple On the Hill"); Paul Dresser ("Just Tell Them That You Saw Me," "I Believe It For My Mother Told Me So"); Edward B. Marks ("My Mother Was a Lady," "The Little Lost Child"); Will Thompson ("Softly and Tenderly," "Gathering Shells From the Seashore").

An even larger number of songs, such as "Wildwood Flower," "Little Rosewood Casket," "Letter Edged in Black," "Put My Little Shoes Away," "The Blind Child," "Two Little Orphans," "Lightning Express," "The East Bound Train," "Over the Garden Wall," "Mary of the Wild Moor," "Jack and Joe," "I'll Be All Smiles Tonight," "Charlie Brooks and Nellie Adair," and "Whisper Your Mother's Name,"[29] came from writers who have been forgotten or who are remembered for only one composition. Students of nineteenth-century pop music may not know the histories of these songs, but fans of old-time country and bluegrass music will easily recognize them. Once imprinted on the song sheets and introduced to the American public, the songs took on lives of their own. We will never know the motives, nor the degree of sincerity, that underlay the writing of those tearful songs of the Victorian era, but generations of rural Southerners have responded to them with compassion and empathy. Writers may have written with tongue in cheek or with a cynical wink at a presumed gullible public,[30] or they may have merely conformed to the conventions of an already proven literary formula. After all, the nostalgic songs of hearth and home had been demonstrating their commercial appeal since the early nineteenth century when John Howard Payne wrote his universally popular "Home

Sweet Home," and when Thomas Moore published his influential songbook *Irish Melodies*. Moore wrote frequently about the "'dream' of sweet security, of a 'home' not too precisely defined, now lost forever in the busy, friendless, risky life of a crowded cosmopolitan city." [31] The southern folk cared not one whit for motivations, nor did they know or care that "The Baggage Coach Ahead" was composed by a black writer named Gussie Davis, or that "Mid the Green Fields of Virginia" was written by Charles K. Harris, a New York Jew who had never been near the Old Dominion State, [32] or that a Connecticut abolitionist named Henry Clay Work had written "Grandfather's Clock," or that a northern minister, George Bennard, had written the beloved gospel song, "The Old Rugged Cross," and that in fact most of their cherished sentimental and parlor songs were conceived in the minds of Yankees. For that matter, their affection for "Dixie," that stirring anthem of southern patriotism, would probably not have dimmed at all had Southerners known that its author was an Ohio-born minstrel entertainer, nor would "Carry Me Back to Old Virginia," which is now that state's official song, have lost its luster among Rebels had they been aware that its creator was a black songwriter from Flushing, Long Island.

The neglected orphans who died in the snow, the heartbroken maidens who died for love, the wandering boys who longed for Mother and Home, the neglected mothers who never stopped dreaming that their wandering boys would come back home, and the brave little boys and girls who rode eastbound trains on lonely expeditions to get their poor blind fathers out of jail were real people to rural Southerners, and they took their places in the hearts and musical repertories of the plain people alongside Lord Thomas and Fair Eleanor, the Gypsy Davy, Barbara Allen, Lord Musgrave, and other venerable heroes from the ancient ballads. Very personal songs of heart-wrenching sentiment coexisted with the older impersonal narratives, with no apparent sense of contradiction on the part of either singers or listeners. There should be no real mystery about the popularity of these more recent songs. Songs like "Letter Edged in Black" and "Lightning Express" preserved the "story" emphasis, and even the complex scheme of subplots (as in "The Fatal Wedding"), of the old ballads. They often conveyed moral or didactic messages, and they appealed to the human need to empathize, even if their ultimate result was merely escape or catharsis. Rural Southerners preserved the basic story lines of the pop songs, and in many cases preserved both melodies and lyrics in forms very close to their published originals. Some songs, however, received substantial alteration as they moved aurally from person to person. As a matter of fact, professional entertainers may have changed the melodic structures and the lyric content of the songs long before they reached the ears of rural listeners. We may never fully understand the social or aesthetic process that governed the selection or rejection of songs, nor the reasons for the changes that were made in their forms.[33] Songs, of course, have been freely altered because an instrumentalist simply could not play the required chords or, as any fan of bluegrass music would know, to give a song greater punch and speed. But the folk also tended to omit those words and chord progressions that seemed needlessly "fancy" or superfluous. In essence, they simplified or "democratized" the songs, making them more singable and acclimated to the values and sensibilities of the folk.

Although the great bulk of nineteenth-century songwriters came from the North, at least one of America's preeminent writers identified with the South and therefore bears a special relationship to its musical culture. He was William Shakespeare Hays, a writer whose career and popularity do much to illuminate the powerful interrelationship between America's folk and popular cultures. Except for a brief stint as a college student in Hanover, Indiana, and at Georgetown in Kentucky, occasional forays as a steamboat pilot on the Ohio River, and a brief sojourn in the Civil War South as a war correspondent, Hays lived out his life between 1837 and 1907 in Louisville, Kentucky.[34] He was passionately devoted to music and had exhibited facile skills as a poet and musician since his teenage years, but, like most writers of his era, he never made music his exclusive profession. His other consuming passion, the great Ohio River that flowed so close to his home, did engage much of his energies throughout his entire life. Hays was for many years the river editor of the *Louisville Courier-Journal*, and his columns were filled with helpful but prosaic details dealing with ship schedules and river conditions. He appears to have been the embodiment of his age's masculine ideal: a rough man with rough and even profane speech, but who exhibited tender sensibilities toward children and women. Idealized visions of women dominated the story lines of many of his best songs, most of which he dedicated to the women he identified on the title sheets.

Hays might best be described as a poet in a poetic age, a period in which popular poetry filled the columns of magazines, small town newspapers, ornately decorated giftbooks, and both privately printed and published volumes. Hays produced at least three small volumes of poetry and songs,[35] along with a large body of songs distributed on sheet music by publishers in Louisville, Cincinnati, and New York. Much like Stephen Foster, to whom he was sometimes compared, Hays prepared different kinds of songs for different markets. Some songs were aimed at that genteel tradition to which Foster had aspired, but most of Hays's compositions were written for the common people, those who received most of their musical sustenance from minstrel entertainment. He wrote songs about war and patriotism (his first successful piece was a song called "The Little Drummer Boy of Shiloh"), political songs (as a conservative but unionist Democrat), topical numbers, a rash of dialect pieces (black, German, Irish, and hayseed), sentimental songs (about mother, children, penniless orphans, and abandoned people), religious songs, southern-oriented songs, and songs about love (both successful and unrequited).[36]

No other writer produced a greater variety of songs than did Hays, and it is doubtful that anyone else's songs enjoyed more extensive circulation, particularly in the twenty years following the Civil War. Several of his songs each sold in the neighborhood of three hundred thousand copies. Historians of popular music, however, pay scant attention to him, or at best provide only grudging recognition. Hazel Meyer, for example, called Hays "the Irving Berlin of his day—in mood and quantity, if not in memorability and quality." On the whole, even those who admit his contemporary popularity treat him as a period piece whose music had no life beyond its own day.[37]

In one sense, music historians cannot be blamed for ignoring what Hays himself seemed not to recognize—that several of his songs took root in the public consciousness and exerted influences in unexpected ways and for periods of time long past the life of their creator. No evidence indicates that Hays knew the extent to which at least a couple of his songs were parodied or plagiarized. He remained genuinely unconcerned about personal profit, and he tried to make his music as widely accessible to the public as possible. He may not have known or cared that his "Little Log Cabin in the Lane" was the inspiration (if not the exact melodic prototype) of such western standards as "Little Old Sod Shanty" and "Little Joe the Wrangler," and even of a song far afield from them all, "Little Red Caboose." Similarly, he may have been unaware that his poem, "The Faithful Engineer," first published in 1886 but later reprinted in 1895 as "Old Hayseed's Railroad Train to Heaven," was the model for one of the South's best loved folk-gospel songs, "Life's Railway to Heaven," a song attributed to M. E. Abbey and Charles Tillman.

Probably the most important reason for the neglect of Hays's historical legacy and that of such writers as Charles K. Harris and Gussie Davis is that popular-music historians simply have not bothered to look beyond the songwriter's own lifetime, or they have not been equipped or predisposed to look into the areas where the music has endured, in the folk tradition and in country music. Neither the scholars of minstrelsy nor of nineteenth-century popular music have been much concerned with the enduring effects of their subjects. Consequently, the documentation of Will Hays's influence on twentieth-century southern music has been left to the folklorists who stumbled onto his songs, or to the students of country music seeking the origins of that form of music. In the early years of the twentieth century, Hays's songs began to show up on the pages of magazines and newspapers, where old and requested songs were printed. They appeared again in "folk song" collections in the late 1910s and early 1920s after Cecil Sharp had made the gathering of folk material seem urgent and respectable. Hays's name, however, appeared much less frequently than did his songs. In 1927, when Carl Sandburg's influential *The American Songbag* was published, a fragment of Hays's "I'll Remember You, Love, in My Prayers" appeared under the title of "When the Curtains of Night are Pinned Back" with the following headnote: "The cowboys of Colorado took a garrulous popular song of the 1870's, and kept a fragment, the heart's essence of it." In the same volume Sandburg obliquely suggested "The Little Old Sod Shanty's" indebtedness to "The Little Log Cabin in the Lane," but he again made no mention of Will Hays.[38]

Hays's songs demonstrated their enduring popular appeal by appearing repeatedly in folk song collections; at least one of them,

"Get in De Middle ob de Road," was published in a Homer Rode-heaver collection of religious songs where it was described as a Negro spiritual![39] "Little Log Cabin in the Lane" was recorded by several musicians around the turn of the century, including the popular opera singer Alma Gluck. In 1923 Hays's songs began a renewed life when "Little (Old) Log Cabin in the Lane," with a slightly altered title, appeared as one side of Fiddlin' John Carson's first Okeh phonograph recording. The surprising popularity of this disc really marked the beginning of country music's commercial history.[40] "Little Log Cabin" began its life in 1871 as the nostalgic complaint of a faithful darkey; by 1923, it had been metamor-phosed into a more general expression of regret about the disappearance of rural society—an impulse that remained central to country music in the decades that followed. Fiddlin' John's rough, backcountry vocal delivery, accompanied only by his fiddle, was far from the genteel performance that Will Hays probably envisioned for his song, but he might have been pleased to learn of the song's endurance. After all, Fiddlin' John had proved that the song belonged to the people.

As country music's commercial history unfolded in the decades after 1923, the central presence in its repertoire of the nineteenth-century popular songs became manifestly clear, and Will Hays's songs reappeared with remarkable regularity. On radio broadcasts and phonograph recordings, in personal appearances, and in song folios such hillbilly singers as Bradley Kincaid, the Carter Family, Ernest Stoneman, Mac and Bob, Karl and Harty, Lula Belle and Scotty, and the Blue Sky Boys introduced Hays's songs to new generations of listeners while simultaneously keeping the music alive for people who were already familiar with it. Such songs as "We Parted by the Riverside," "You've Been a Friend to Me," "I'll Remember You, Love, in My Prayers," "Mollie Darling," and "Nobody's Darling on Earth" easily reinforced the emphasis on home and parlor—the moral impulse—which remained part of country music's self-defining image in the decades following its commercial birth. John Lair, the genial and nostalgic radio personality and promoter, began resurrecting these songs, and other vintage numbers like them, in the early 1930s, first in his capacity as music librarian for the "National Barn Dance" radio program in Chicago, and later as the host of his own creation, the "Renfro Valley Barn Dance" in Kentucky.[41] To Lair, these were not simply old songs; they were instead remnants of an older and valued way of life that was fast disappearing.

Although these early country versions of Hays's songs exhibited the enduring appeal of Victorian music and the value scheme it embodied, none of them could be described as commercially successful. However, they have inspired a continuing stream of recordings by later generations of commercial country performers. In 1990, for example, the Whitstein Brothers, an old-time-oriented duet from Alexandria, Louisiana, recorded a version of "We Parted by the Riverside" modeled clearly on an earlier performance by the Blue Sky Boys.[42] On both recordings the song carried no composer credits, but was described as being in the public domain.

The immediate source of Eddy Arnold's 1946 recording of "Molly Darling" is unknown, but the tremendous popularity of Arnold's performance cannot be doubted. He clearly won a larger audience for this song than Hays was ever able to gain for any of his compositions. The song, of course, also played a major role in securing Arnold's position as the number-one country star in postwar America.[43] Lester Flatt and Earl Scruggs's version of "Jimmie Brown the Newsboy," on the other hand, very likely derived from an earlier Carter Family performance, and it was generally assumed that A. P. Carter had either written the song or adapted it from an older number in the public domain. The song was in fact a product of someone's rather freewheeling adaptation of Will Hays's "Jimmie Brown the Paper Boy," written in 1875. Shorn of some of its more ponderous and saccharine phraseology, and performed to the melodic and syncopated beat of Earl Scruggs's guitar, the song became a standard of bluegrass music. No Will Hays song has been more often performed.[44]

Bluegrass musicians still occasionally resurrect "Jimmie Brown the Newsboy" or "Little Old Log Cabin in the Lane," and old-time musicians like the Whitstein Brothers or Ramona and Alisa Jones still perform versions of other Hays songs such as "We Parted by the Riverside" or "Shamus O'Brien."[45] Other pop sounds from earlier centuries continue to make their way into the performances of country musicians. Hornpipes that were danced in seventeenth- and eighteenth-century Britain, or on the concert stages of early America, as well as minstrel and ragtime pieces from the first great flowering of American popular entertainment, even yet appear in the repertories of country fiddlers. Septimus Winner's "Listen to the Mockingbird" survives as a showpiece for fiddlers, and Henry Clay Work's "Grandfather's Clock" has become an instrumental piece prized by bluegrass banjo players. Both of those genteel composers might be shocked at the abandon with which their once-sentimental songs are now performed, but they could not be displeased at their endurance and widespread appeal. Singers like Mac Wiseman, Doc Watson, and Grandpa Jones also keep alive songs like "Letter Edged in Black," "Little Rosewood Casket," "Put My Little Shoes Away," "Baldheaded End of the Broom," and other survivals of early Tin Pan Alley.

To most popular-music historians, these songs are obscure and largely trivial relics of America's first great commercial flirtation with mass culture. If mentioned at all by such historians, they are discussed airily or with tongue in cheek, and dismissed in the condescending fashion of Sigmund Spaeth who called them "songs we forgot to remember."[46] They are assumed to have been little more than the passing fancies of our naive forebears, and to have had no lives past the immediate years of their initial publications. But any student of country music should know that, while their writers may have been forgotten, the songs have lived, and have been remembered. We may call them "folk songs," but to the real "folk" who have preserved, revived, and performed them, they have been simply old and good songs. In Bradley Kincaid's day, when the country music business was still taking shape, they were part of the cluster of "old-familiar tunes" that were known by most rural Southerners. They were, in truth, "songs my mama used to sing." Some years later, as the increasingly commercialized country music industry generated its own traditions, these surviving songs might be explained as "old songs I used to hear Bradley Kincaid sing on WLS radio." And even later, perhaps during the folk revival of the 1960s when a renewed interest in old songs became apparent among young people throughout the nation, such a song might be described as a "Flatt and Scruggs song" or as "one of my favorite Mac Wiseman songs" (even though these musicians may have learned such material from older commercial sources). To be sure, some of the more sophisticated students within the folk revival, especially those with academic experience, recognized the ages of the songs and often used the term "folk" to describe them. But only rarely have the names Will S. Hays, Charles K. Harris, Gussie Davis, Henry Clay Work, Paul Dresser, or any of the other lesser lights of Tin Pan Alley been admitted into the discussions of the songs' origins. Nor does one find much recognition of the powerful roles played in the creation and dissemination of such music by some long-forgotten broadside ballad vendor, equestrian hornpipe dancer, puppet show fiddler, medicine show banjoist, showboat band, minstrel tenor, singing circus clown, ragtime pianist, or vaudeville vocalist. This selective list of entertainers represents a tradition of popular entertainment that long antedates the history of the United States, and one that has always been intimately interrelated with the lives and culture of the folk. The southern people did not "forget to remember" the music, comedy, and dance that flowed from these varied forums of popular entertainment. Simultaneously "folk" and "popular," the musical heritage bequeathed by this tradition constituted one of the great bedrocks of the early country music business. Remembered and revered, this music continues to enrich the repertories of many of the musicians of our own time.

Chapter Three

Mountaineers and Cowboys: Country Music's Search for Identity

The rural music that began to appear on radio broadcasts and phonograph recordings in the early 1920s resisted precise definition. The men and women who made the music, as fiddlers, banjoists, string bands, gospel singers, yodelers, and balladeers, came from many communities in the South and Midwest, and they represented a wide variety of localized musical expressions. Their music clearly conveyed the flavor, tone, and dialects of grassroots America, but, as we have seen, it was not totally rural in either source or manifestation. Furthermore, as incipient professional musicians they had no models of show business success within their own communities. The only touchstones of achievement, or objects of emulation, came from minstrelsy, vaudeville, and other forms of organized entertainment. The early country musicians were, preponderantly, workers and farmers who performed music as an avocation. Some of them never sought more than a part-time diversion from textile work, railroading, coal mining, farming, or whatever economic calling consumed their lives. Others, however, seized upon music as an escape from working-class life and, like most Americans, defined success in terms of the middle-class ideal. Early promotional photographs of country musicians almost invariably show them dressed in their "Sunday-go-to-meeting" clothes—suits, ties, well-polished shoes—and not in overalls, brogans, blue jeans, or other accoutrements of working-class life. The musicians were rural and working class, but they saw no immediate incentive to "package" themselves in such a fashion.

If this "new" form of music could not be easily defined, neither could it be conveniently labeled. The music industry groped for terms that might encapsulate the diverse styles and songs that ranged from the lonesome balladry of the Kentucky hills to the wild string band music of North Georgia and the cowboy harmonies of Texas. The Columbia record label probably came closest to accuracy when it described its catalogue of rural music (the 15,000–D Series) as "Old Familiar Tunes." But even that label obviously could not be used forever as the music developed into an industry with self-conscious performers and independent writers who sought fresh and original material. The pioneer performers had no clear self-identity, nor a distinct conviction of what the American public would buy or accept. Hence, the mood of uncertainty and self-deprecation encountered in Al Hopkins, the leader of a string band from Virginia and North Carolina, when he replied to the recording entrepreneur Ralph Peer: "Just call us anything you want, we're nothing but a bunch of hillbillies."[1] Probably neither Hopkins nor any other early country entertainer deliberately sought the image or label of "hillbilly" or any identification that suggested backwardness or a musical style that lay outside the mainstream of American respectability. No pioneer country musician really sought to identify with "rural" or "working-class" life; even the personas of the "railroad man," the "hobo," and the "cowboy," roles that some country musicians assumed, were associated more with life-style than with work. Certainly no country entertainer could have anticipated immediately the appeal that certain images from rural and working-class life later evoked among the American public.

Early country musicians, however, did not perform in a cultural vacuum. They presented their music to an American public that already possessed a cluster of perceptions—largely romantic and often contradictory—about the South, rural life, folk culture, and folk music. If they pondered such subjects at all, most Americans thought of "southern folk music"[2] as an amalgam of black spirituals and Stephen Foster melodies, or as a body of ancient ballads that had found sanctuary in the remote recesses of the southern Appalachians. Americans had long had a love-hate relationship with their rural past, alternately romanticizing or rejecting it;[3] this ambivalence was only heightened in the 1920s when all of our rural values seemed threatened by a burgeoning technological dominance. Rural southern whites in that same decade were viewed through a similarly distorted lens, often as degenerate hayseeds (the kind of people who gaped and guffawed at the Scopes trial), or as victims of a retrogressive economic system, and only rarely as a people whose culture was worth commemorating. Mountaineers were sometimes idealized as a sturdy individualistic people who clung to Elizabethan folkways, and cowboys, from the western edge of the South, were beginning to share a comparable mythicization. Other rural Southerners, who presumably made no music at all, suffered from a general stigma not far removed from that described by H. L. Mencken in his famous essay of 1920, "Sahara of the Bozart." Largely because of the Civil War, he argued, the South had been "drained of all its best blood," leaving the land to "the harsh mercies of the poor white trash" in whose veins flowed "the worst blood of Western Europe."[4]

It is tempting to say that the commercial fraternity was neutral in its attitudes toward the folk, and that merchandisers of products (whether music or soap) did not know or care if the "folk" were Elizabethan, backwards, or anything else. If a potential market for grassroots music could be discerned, they would exploit it, without concern for its art, or the lack of it. Few merchandisers were as frank or cynical as the correspondent who wrote an article for *Etude* magazine in 1934. This self-described "dealer in sound-reproducing machines" to rural Southerners depicted his customers as a childlike people who lived in a musical "underworld."[5] We know, though, that while the commercial fraternity thought mainly of profits, the recording men, radio executives, publicists, promoters, ad men, sponsors, and booking agents who dealt with folk music also readily manipulated symbols, images, and public perceptions in order to sell their products. The businessmen were no more immune to visions of isolated mountain coves, wind-swept deserts, little cabin homes, and country churches than was the public who listened to the music. Like Ralph Peer, who affixed the term "hillbilly" to some of the records he produced, or George D. Hay of the "WSM Barn Dance," who encouraged his entertainers to wear overalls and gingham dresses while giving them names like Possum Hunters and Fruit Jar Drinkers, or like the songbook illustrators who linked the music to certain visual rustic images,[6] the businessmen contributed vitally to the public perceptions of this developing musical form.

Although "hillbilly" became a universally used rubric to describe virtually every form of country music, and is still used privately by many performers to describe themselves, it was never a satisfying public label for those who sought mainstream acceptance. Until the neutral and relatively respectable term "country" won general usage in the mid 1940s, the musicians and their promoters resorted most often to the exploitation of images surrounding two of America's most romantic groups: mountaineers and cowboys. In the same period in American history, running roughly from 1880 to 1910, cowboys, mountaineers and their music were "discovered" and "memorialized" in the context of a national hunger and nostalgia for simpler times and a simpler society. Like the Cajuns, Creoles, "faithful" ex-slaves, and other "exotic" elements who appeared in the local color and travel literature in the waning years of the nineteenth century, mountaineers and cowboys exerted a relatively benign influence on an increasingly literate public, which sought greater knowledge of the world that lay beyond its own doorsteps. Although clothed in romance, and often vested with virtually unreadable dialects by their authors, the characters found in the novels and short stories, on the silver screen, or in other expressions of popular culture, provided some education and much diversion for American audiences. Some readers and spectators, however, may have been motivated, either consciously or unconsciously, by more than simple diversion or entertainment and may have gravitated toward exotic rustic types through a reaction against the massive social alterations that were changing the face of a once familiar America. Mountaineers and cowboys were not simply colorful and exotic; they were vivid reminders of frontier America and of the allegedly individualistic traits that had once characterized American life. Unlike most of the other local-color characters, mountaineers and cowboys had the additional advantage of being "Anglo-Saxon," a deeply satisfying attribute to many people who viewed with regret the inundation of the nation by "new" and perhaps unassimilable immigrants. Furthermore, mountaineers and cowboys valued, and presumably embodied, freedom and independence; both were heroic and fearless; both preserved those manly traits that had ensured survival on the frontier and that were distinctive and defining ingredients of American life. Cowboys and mountaineers, in short, were profoundly American.

When country music began its commercial development in the early 1920s, images of cowboys and mountaineers were already present in American popular culture, and songs associated with each group were familiar to at least a small coterie of scholars and concert performers. Small and sometimes privately printed collections had been appearing since the turn of the century, but John A. Lomax's *Cowboy Songs and Other Frontier Ballads*, published in 1910, and Cecil Sharp's *English Folksongs from the Southern Appalachians*, published in 1917, did most to make Americans aware of such music.[7] It is impossible to know how many of the songs from these volumes were known by early country musicians, but no one—whether musician, promoter, or fan—could have been unaware of the potent appeal of cowboy and mountain images. In the seven decades of its history, country music has exhibited a symbiotic relationship with cowboys and mountaineers. The music has drawn persistently upon images associated with these powerful cultural figures for sustenance, definition, and identity, but has in turn done much to shape popular conceptions of these romantic symbols. It may be merely an accident, but the first documented southern rural musician to appear on a phonograph recording, Eck Robertson, dressed like a cowboy when he journeyed to New York in 1922 for his audition. Robertson was born in Arkansas, but had been living in the Texas Panhandle near Amarillo for several years before he made the trip to New York. He certainly would have been familiar and comfortable with western attire because of his Texas residence, but he also would not have been unaware of the cowboys who had long been appearing in Wild West Shows and in silent films. Robertson had been a popular and successful performer at fiddle contests and country dances for most of his life. And while we do not know how he dressed at such events, "the cowboy as performer," if not as a musician, would certainly have been familiar to him.[8]

While Eck Robertson provided an early glimpse of the equating of "cowboy" and "music," and anticipated what would become an overpowering and irresistible impulse in the 1930s, the mountaineer initially exerted the strongest impact on the emerging country music field. Despite the excessive romanticization and consequent distortion of the concept of "mountain music," mountain people nevertheless did make music. In recalling his sojourn in the southern Appalachians, Cecil Sharp had said "I found myself for the first time in my life in a community in which singing was as common and almost as universal a practice as speaking."[9] Like the initial forays made by the ballad collectors, most of the early commercial recording expeditions journeyed to the southeastern United States, lured there because of the relative ease of travel from New York, but also perhaps because of romantic visions planted earlier by local colorists, cultural missionaries, and folk song collectors. Texas, on the other hand, was far away, and except for the "ranch dances" that often stilled the pangs of loneliness and isolation, a culture of cowboy music did not exist. It was yet to be manufactured by the commercial revolution unleashed by the phonograph, radio, and motion picture.

Robertson's initial recordings in 1922 were unadvertised and unmarketed, but the next year Fiddlin' John Carson, who claimed the North Georgia hills as his birthplace, made his first records for the Okeh label. The surprising popularity of Fiddlin' John's recordings inspired a similar exploitation of other rural entertainers by the record industry. The bulk of these performers came from the Southeast, and many of them actually came from the mountains. Carson came from somewhere in North Georgia, either in or near the mountains, but no documentation provides conclusive evidence of either his birthplace or the exact date of his birth (estimates range from 1868 to 1874).[10] By the time of his first recording in 1923, Carson was far removed from his origins in the hills of northeast Georgia, and was living in a working-class suburb of Atlanta known as "Cabbagetown," a neighborhood defined by the Fulton Bag and Cotton Mill. Early publicity brochures did make passing reference to his mill employment, but none mentioned his Cabbagetown residence even though he had lived there since 1900. He was instead described as a product of the North Georgia mountains, with the little community of Blue Ridge, in Fannin County, described most often as his birthplace. We do not know what underlay the descriptions made of Carson by journalists and by his record company, nor the degree to which Carson influenced the building of his public image. Fiddlin' John and his publicists, however, surely knew about John Fox, Jr.'s, romantic novels of Appalachia, and about the hit song of 1913, "Trail of the Lonesome Pine," which had referred to the "blue ridge mountains of Virginia."[11] Like many transplanted rural Southerners, Fiddlin' John's heart and music remained moored to the hills of home, and he may have instinctively known that a multitude of Americans also yearned for those hills, at least symbolically, and were prepared to journey there on the wings of song.

The lure of the mountains was almost irresistible for music industry image makers, country musicians, and their fans. But while "mountain music" became one of the many designations used to describe early country music, the term "mountain" did not convey the same meaning to all who were attracted to it. While the image of a remote and romantic land filled with a peculiarly musical and racially pure people was broadly appealing, the mountaineer and his music also evoked negative responses. Consequently, the depictions of mountaineers and mountain life in country music, as expressed in songs, costumes, comedy, publicity, and performing titles, ranged from burlesque, ridicule, and self-parody to romance and sentimentality. Whether the performers actually came from the mountains or not, both they and their commercial managers were probably aware of the popular and literary conceptions of mountaineers and, above all, of the supposed linkage of "mountaineers" and "music." Some early depictions of mountaineers in country music stressed the alleged "moral" qualities of mountain life, or concentrated on nostalgic longings for the old "mountain home," but just as many others centered upon the quaint, silly, or perverse aspects of mountain existence. When record publicity notes and journalistic accounts described Fiddlin' John Carson as a "moonshiner," or referred to his Atlanta-born daughter, Rosa Lee, as "Moonshine Kate," the usually unnamed publicist could not have been unaware of the public association of the whiskey-making art with mountain culture. In 1925 recording scout Ralph Peer had inadvertently given a name to the developing country music industry when he labeled Al Hopkins's group of musicians from the southern hills as "the Hillbillies." The Hillbillies, who soon described themselves as the "Original Hillbillies" when other groups appropriated the name, were featured in a fifteen-minute film for Warner Brothers sometime in 1927.[12] Made during a brief vaudeville tour in New York and the Northeast, the film portrayed the band members doing incredibly silly things and playing frenetically upon their respective instruments. "Hillbilly" was a term that could encompass all kinds of backwoods inhabitants, but the film documented the musicians wearing costumes associated with mountain life. The group clearly responded to a public conception of the hillbilly as a comic or laughable character.

The hillbilly stage comedian, of course, was but the manifestation of a much older comic depiction of the rustic person, a tradition seen as early as Shakespeare, and one which had appeared frequently in vaudeville, burlesque, and other forms of popular

entertainment. Historically, the character had seldom been identified with the mountains, but instead reeked of the backwoods.
Cal Stewart's rural stage and recording persona, Uncle Josh, presumably could have lived in any small town in the United States,
while Toby, the country bumpkin of the tent repertoire shows,
tended to be a character with no clear regional identity. In the
years following the birth of commercial country music, the hillbilly personality, both comic and serious, became linked more
directly to public images of mountaineers and mountain culture.
The show business hillbilly, however, was not simply a reflection
of public perceptions dealing with mountain life; the character
also did much to shape or to strengthen those perceptions.

The hillbilly/mountain emphasis asserted itself in a variety of
ways during the years following 1925. The "L'il Abner" comic
strip, introduced in 1934, which presented its version of hillbilly
life to millions of Americans each day, apparently was inspired
directly by a hillbilly music vaudeville act. The strip's creator, Al
Capp, had seen some years earlier an unnamed hillbilly troupe
in New York and was fascinated by their music and droll humor.
That experience, and a hike soon thereafter through the southern Appalachians, influenced his decision to create the cartoon
series.[13] The hillbilly act may have been Al Hopkins's band, or
it could have been one of several similar acts that appeared on
New York stages by the end of the 1920s. The Weaver Brothers
and Elviry, for example, were a group of musicians and comedians from the Missouri Ozarks who were mainstays in vaudeville
and B movies throughout the 1920s and 1930s. Through its appearances in northern vaudeville houses, the Weaver group built
an audience among people who otherwise had little or no contact with country music acts.[14] Other hillbilly performers, like
Lum and Abner, Bob Burns (an Ozark comedian who told jokes
and played a homemade instrument called a bazooka), and Judy

Canova, had only tenuous connections to the country music world, but they reached a huge American audience with their versions of hillbilly humor. Country music played little or no role in these national radio broadcasts. Canova, for example, spoke with a country twang and sometimes featured a skit about Ma and Pa, a slow-talking and slow-thinking mountain couple, but her musical selections were almost always chosen from the current roster of pop hits.

The flirtation with "mountain" names, songs, and humor has reappeared from time to time in mainstream pop music since the days of Judy Canova. The imagery and themes have sometimes been evocatively romantic, as in John Denver's "Country Roads" or Judy Collins's "The Coming of the Roads," but most often the treatment has reinvoked hackneyed stereotypes about mountain life and culture. Such songs have ranged from the relatively innocuous "I Like Mountain Music" to "The Martins and the Coys," "Zeb Turney's Girl," "Feudin', Fussin', and a-Fightin'" (all about the venerable tradition of feuding), "Slap Her Down Again, Pa," and "Good Old Mountain Dew" (a perennial fraternity party favorite). Much of this material came from Tin Pan Alley and was performed by singers like Dorothy Shay, the Broadway-style performer of the 1940s who was billed as "the Park Avenue Hillbilly."

Although the impulse toward self-burlesque and parody remained strong in country music—as witnessed by the remarkable success of the "Hee Haw" television show in the 1970s—a countervailing desire to stress the dignity of mountain life also constantly asserted itself. A few performers in the first commercial decade, including Bascom Lamar Lunsford, Buell Kazee, the Carter Family, and Bradley Kincaid, appropriated positive images of mountain life rooted in a society of traditional values—images of morality, stability, and home-centeredness—and used them in their songs, styles, and stage personae. Lunsford had a long and distinguished career as a lawyer, performer, and folk music promoter; he was the organizer of the oldest, and most influential, folk festival in the United States, the Mountain Dance and Folk Festival founded in 1928 in Asheville, North Carolina, as part of that city's Rhododendron Festival. While laboring to preserve the most authentic specimens of traditional song and style in his native western North Carolina, Lunsford also maintained a relationship with commercial hillbilly music, and he recorded a large number of folk songs for both the Library of Congress and commercial recording companies.[15]

Buell Kazee, from Magoffin County, Kentucky, made only a few commercial recordings, but he lived long enough to enjoy a renewed career during the "folk revival" of the 1960s. During his brief tenure on records, Kazee's recording company, Brunswick, advertised him as a mountain boy, and though he sometimes recorded songs that exploited the pejorative or stereotypical images of violence and wildness (as in "Wild Bill Jones" and "Old Moonshiner"), he tended generally to play a role that befitted his background of college study and ministerial work. Kazee learned in his literature courses at Georgetown College that many of the songs he grew up with had "ancient" origins and were linked to the oldest traditions of British poetry. Regardless of the type of song he chose to perform, Kazee presented the material with great dignity and seriousness, in a manner reflecting both his view of mountain culture and his lifelong commitment to the Baptist ministry.[16]

Like Kazee, the Virginia-born Carter Family (A. P., his wife Sara, and their sister-in-law Maybelle) were of genuine mountain origin, but unlike him they had no college training and few pretensions to high culture. There seems to have been no one in their reference group, and certainly no professors of English literature, who might have influenced their performance of British balladry or their conceptions of mountain culture. On the other hand, they launched their professional career at a time when rather vague, but romantic, notions about mountain life prevailed. No real evidence suggests that either the Carter Family or Ralph Peer, the talent scout who first recorded them, made any conscious attempt to exploit explicit mountain imagery. Peer, however, did suggest that they record old songs, and the Carters were predisposed to perform such material and in a style reminiscent of family gatherings around the fireside. The Carters' repertory, their style of singing, and the general mood that they conveyed in their concerts—"this program is morally good"—conveyed the flavor of the *rural* Victorian South. But given the context of the 1920s, when the lowland rural South suffered from a multitude of evils both real and imagined (sharecropping, pellagra, illiteracy, racial bigotry, moral degeneracy),[17] it was tempting to equate the Carter style with the allegedly more pristine mountain image. The Carter Family's image, repertory, and style of performance affected the perceptions of both performers and fans for many years to follow.

The Carters sang quite a few songs, either taken from "tradition" or "made up" by A. P. himself, that commented on or paid tribute to their mountain homes: "My Old Clinch Mountain Home," "Foggy Mountain Top," "Longing For Old Virginia," "Mid the Green Fields of Virginia," and others. The Carters left their Virginia homes in 1938 to relocate in Del Rio, Texas, where they began a series of transcribed shows on the powerful Mexican broadcasting station, XERA.[18] Far from the Clinch Mountains, and with A. P. and Sara's strained marriage already past the breaking point, the Carter Family continued to sing about the values and virtues of the old rural home. When the Carters sang about those "green fields of Virginia far away," few listeners would have known or cared that the lyrics had been written many years earlier by a Jewish composer who had not been to the Old Dominion

State when he committed his thoughts to paper. On the contrary, for the many people who heard the Carter Family broadcasts in the vast territory touched by XERA's transmission, the song was simply a vehicle through which one found communion with the peacefulness, contentment, stability and other presumed values of mountain life.

While mountain life was evoked in their programs and songs, the Carter Family did not depend exclusively on such identification. Bradley Kincaid, on the other hand, built his career around the image of a mountain boy singing to an audience of city people. He consciously styled himself as "the Kentucky Mountain Boy," and constantly referred to his music as "mountain music." [19]

By the time Kincaid made his first broadcasts on WLS in Chicago in 1927, his audiences may already have been sufficiently predisposed to think of the southern Appalachians as the home of a quaint and old-fashioned people and as a repository of old songs and ballads. Few listeners would have heard of Cecil Sharp, but many would have been familiar with John Fox, Jr.'s, novels about the Kentucky mountains, and even more would have known the story of Sgt. Alvin York, the Tennessee mountain boy who became the most decorated hero of World War I. Kincaid was from Kentucky, and he sang what were described as "folk songs." It was therefore easy for his program director to affix the label "mountain boy" to him, and it was just as easy for his listeners in the North and Midwest to equate "Kentucky" with "mountains."

While public perceptions were important in inspiring Kincaid's identification with mountain roots, his longtime affiliation with Berea College, in the foothills of Kentucky's Cumberland Mountains, was probably more important in welding his links with a mountain heritage. Kincaid had great affection for and loyalty to this historic school whose primary department he had entered in 1914 at the age of nineteen (he entered at the sixth grade level and, after a two-year stint in the U.S. Army, received his high school diploma). Imbued with the mission of educating and uplifting the mountain children who matriculated at Berea, Kincaid's teachers inculcated him with the precepts of Christian service and middle-class morality. Teachers like his English instructor, John Smith, who were much influenced by the academic folk song tradition of Francis James Child and Cecil Sharp, introduced him to ballad literature. His Berea instruction, and the Berea mystique, encouraged him to think of his music as "mountain music" and of that music as a product of a moral culture. In his collections of radio songs, issued under the sponsorship of WLS, Kincaid spoke disparagingly of "hillybilly [sic] and bum songs," and extolled the mountain folk from whom he had obtained his songs as "a people in whose veins runs the purest strain of Anglo-Saxon blood." [20]

Kincaid circulated what he liked to describe as "southern mountain songs," first on the "WLS Barn Dance," and then on a succession of radio stations throughout the Midwest and New England. Despite the descriptions he affixed to himself and his music, Kincaid was no "mountain boy." He was from Paint Lick, Kentucky— as near to the bluegrass region as it is to the mountains. On occasion Kincaid's actions bespoke a borderlander's ambiguity. He sometimes wore leather riding boots and jodhpurs, the attire of English foxhunters, and the garb affected by bluegrass gentlemen horsemen. In 1941, while at WHAM in Rochester, New York, he began wearing cowboy clothes while hosting his own show called the "Circle B Ranch." Kincaid's music also represented a wide assortment of songs, both traditional and popular. He was correct in arguing that many of his songs were known and loved by mountain people, but such songs were neither exclusive nor necessarily indigenous to the mountains. Folklorist Archie Green claims that Kincaid "pioneered by bringing Appalachian folksong to national radio audiences," while Kincaid's principal biographer, Loyal Jones, asserts that he "was the first artist to become a radio star using almost entirely authentic folk music."[21] More precisely, Kincaid's music was composed of a substantial body of old-time, or "old familiar," songs known throughout much of rural America, as well as a significant assortment of obscure or original items, like "Some Little Bug Is Going to Find You" and "Legend of the Robin Red Breast," that were *introduced* to the folk. Kincaid tried to lend respectability to his music by associating it with an image of Appalachian mountain folk drawn largely from his Berea experience, the conception of an ethnically pure and morally virtuous people who valued tradition. Archie Green maintains that Kincaid's contributions had lasting implications: "Our very conception today, that much American folksong is by definition undefiled, a precious elixir for national well-being, stems in part from Bradley Kincaid's achievement."[22]

For many people caught up in the fascination with the southern mountains, neither the Carter Family nor Bradley Kincaid were satisfactory musical embodiments; nor would any country singer be acceptable who came after them. The "mountain" singers of radio and recording, that is, the hillbillies, represented a world and way of life that did not conform to the image of mountain life embraced by most academicians and concert singers of folk songs: that of a static and nonpecuniary society. The "hillbilly business," so it was believed, was a tawdry world of show business and money grubbing. The music disseminated by the radio singers dealt similarly with themes and issues—often sentimentalized— that seldom squared with the intellectualized or ethereal view of mountain culture. Some apostles of folk music refused to truckle with the marketplace and therefore rejected every manifestation of commercial popularization. Folk scholars, for the most part, clung to a literary conception of folk music, and preserved the ideal of Child ballads sung in the modal style. They perceived hillbilly music as an enemy that was infiltrating the hills and seducing the children of the mountain folk. The literary-oriented folklorists tended to keep their attentions focused on scholarship, and, while they might actually go "into the field" to collect ballads, they made few efforts to present the music to an audience through either concerts or records. A few collectors, however, followed the entrepreneurial path pioneered by Alan Lomax, and by the end of the 1940s they had begun to introduce traditional mountain singers like Texas Gladden and Horton Barker to urban and academic audiences. Still others, like Bascom Lamar Lunsford, Jean Thomas, Sarah Gertrude Knott, and John Powell, worked principally through the venue of the folk festival and argued that the performance of folk music, mountain or otherwise, was acceptable only if done by the real "folk" and in "premodern" styles. Still another coterie of ballad collectors, some of whom sought to use folk music as the basis of a truly national form of art music, tried to link the performance of such music to the cultivated or art tradition, a phenomenon that began in the World War I period with such concert musicians as Edna Thomas, Loraine Wyman, and Howard Brockway.[23]

The concert performers of folk music, and their patrons, took great pains to distinguish their "mountain folk songs" from the "hillbilly songs" of the radio performers. When John Jacob Niles brought his dulcimer to Cincinnati in September 1938 to present a program of "mountain songs" at the Hyde Park Country Club, the Queen City's radio stations were already hosts to a wide variety of hillbilly acts, including two of the nation's most popular barn dances, the "Renfro Valley Barn Dance" and the "Boone County Jamboree." Niles's sponsors, the American Association of University Women, were probably thinking of such musicians when they assured his potential audience that Niles was a "true musician," not a hillbilly singer.[24]

Niles, of course, was neither a mountain nor hillbilly singer; like Loraine Wyman and other concert musicians who preceded him, he was an artistic "interpreter" of folk music. Jean Ritchie, on the other hand, fulfilled every expectation of both the concert and academic folk music fraternities, and she effectively created an alliance between the two groups. Ritchie was a genuine mountain girl who grew up in a family of folk singers in the little Cumberland Mountain community of Viper in Perry County, Kentucky.[25] Until she began writing songs, Ritchie's music essentially was that which came from her family—parents and older relatives, and her sisters. Her concerts and recordings, though, tended to concentrate on a select and specialized list of songs— the rarest and presumably oldest of her family's songs. Ritchie's role as a cultural missionary for mountain music came, in large part, through the patronage of Alan Lomax, who in 1948 arranged her first concert bookings and recordings (for the Library of Congress). Recording for a public audience after 1950, beginning with the Elektra label, she wittingly or unwittingly gave listeners the impression that her repertory represented the full range of her family's music, and that such music represented the totality of mountain music. She did not simply present the musical history of her family; she presented that which was "best," and that which was calculated to win the favor of her articulate, middle-class, and largely nonsouthern audience. Like Woody Guthrie, who also traveled to New York to find an audience for his special brand of folk music, Ritchie embodied the traditions of the southern folk. It was the fate of both singers, however, to carve out performing identities far away from the folk communities that gave them birth and among audiences that were predisposed to think of folk music and folk singers in special symbolic ways.

Folklorist D. K. Wilgus was apparently the first scholar to note that the Ritchie sisters popularized a "settlement school" tradition of folk music[26]—a body of songs learned from their teachers and classmates in such mountain settlement schools as Hindman and Pine Mountain—and then succeeded in convincing many of their listeners that such music was the most authentic and indigenous representation of mountain culture. Ironically, Jean, to her great regret, did not attend the settlement schools—she went instead to the first public school established in her county—but she learned songs that her older sisters brought home from the settlements. D. K. Wilgus argued that the Ritchies' music, as winnowed out and interpreted by the talented Jean in her public performances, created a misleading impression about the breadth and nature of mountain music. David Whisnant goes even further and argues that much of the Ritchies' music, like the folk dances popularized by the settlement schools and by Berea College, was not indigenous to the mountains but was imported by cultural uplifters who hoped to elevate the morals of their students while also holding back the tide of modernization represented by hillbilly music.[27]

Ritchie has since acknowledged that her selections of songs may have unwittingly contributed to a narrowly focused view of Appalachian folk music. In the notes to a 1960s recording, *Precious Memories*, and in the songs included there, she noted that she and her sisters had known some of the radio hillbilly songs—such as "Picture on the Wall" and "Rosewood Casket." And she declared that "it is to set the record straight, to present a truer picture of singing in the southern mountains, that I have come to undertake this program of songs."[28] Ritchie clouds the issue, however, when she alleges that the radio first introduced new and alien songs and styles (i.e., hillbilly) in the 1920s. Pop songs and gospel hymns had been moving into the mountains, and into the hearts of a receptive people (including her own) long before then. Most important, Ritchie's superb autobiography, *Singing Family of the Cumberlands*, reveals much more than she probably intended.

She indicates, for example, that alternative musical ideas came into the Ritchie household very early in the twentieth century. Her father, Balis, had bought a secondhand printing press before Jean was born, and in addition to a weekly newspaper he also published a songbook with a title that suggested a greater breadth of musical interest than that conveyed in her concerts: *Lover's Melodies, A Choice Collection of Old Sentimental Songs Our Grandmothers Sang, and Other Popular Airs.* The book did contain some of the old ballads, but it also included material like "Kitty Wells" and "Casey Jones." Balis clearly did not shun innovation. In about 1905, he and his brother Isaac walked eighty miles to Jackson, Kentucky, to pick up a new cylinder talking machine they had ordered from Sears, Roebuck. Few other rural Southerners would have experienced the delights of a record player at such an early date.[29]

Whatever her inclinations or motives, Jean Ritchie did reaffirm, for a large segment of people, the specialized and esoteric conception of Appalachian music first promulgated by Cecil Sharp and the early collectors and reinforced by the settlement schools and Berea College and their tradition of moral uplift. Perceived as a rather gentle music performed with lilting voice and delicate dulcimer, Appalachian music called forth visions of Elizabethan purity and pristine isolation. Ritchie's version of Appalachian music was honest, true to her personal roots, and faithfully performed; but it represented only one facet of a much larger and infinitely more complex musical culture. People who attended Ritchie's concerts or bought her records did not simply experience a musical performance that seemed frozen in time, but one that had also been sheltered from the social and technological transformations that had been sweeping across the mountains since long before she was born.[30]

While the warring images of "hillbilly" and "mountaineer" contested for the allegiance of both performers and fans, the "cow-boy" image aggressively and persistently enveloped the country music field. Neither cowboys nor cowboy songs had been totally absent from the early country music business. Cowboy songs had been appearing on phonograph recordings since 1919 when concert singer Bentley Ball, in a stilted and highly affected style, sang "The Dying Cowboy" and "Jesse James." When the hillbilly music business began its evolution in the 1920s, a few cowboy singers—some of whom, like Jules Verne Allen and Harry McClintock, had actually done ranch work—commercially recorded a handful of songs. Still others began to appear on radio stations during that decade. These included the New Yorker, John White, who sang as "The Lonesome Cowboy" while presenting the true story of each song to his radio listeners.[31] The cowboy genre was not as immediately appealing to classical musicians as was the Appalachian style, but a few composers, such as Oscar Fox, David Guion and, preeminently, Aaron Copland, nevertheless did experiment with cowboy music, and some of them found John Lomax's song-book to be an indispensable source. At least one of these compositions won national exposure outside the concert hall when Guion's arrangement of "Home on the Range" became identified with President Franklin Roosevelt, who declared it to be his favorite song.

The first anticipation of the powerful role that the cowboy mystique would play in country music came during the career of Jimmie Rodgers. Rodgers, the Mississippi railroad brakeman who became country music's first star, recorded a diverse repertory of songs that included at least seven cowboy numbers. Prior to the date of his first Victor recordings in August 1927, Rodgers had spent much time in the Appalachian spa of Asheville, North Carolina, where he sought relief from the tuberculosis that ravaged most of his adult life. But if Rodgers absorbed any of the mountain mystique that had so captivated Cecil Sharp and others, one finds no evidence in his music nor in his stage persona. Like most of the country performers who came after him, Rodgers turned his gaze westward, and was drawn irresistibly toward the image of the man on horseback. The cowboy made a marked impact on Rodgers's dress, and on his choice of songs.[32] In Rodgers's mind and songs, the cowboy may have meshed easily with the rambler, a figure traditionally venerated by the folk because of his bold assertion of freedom. But to a degree much stronger than the rootless rambler, the cowboy, unrestrained by the confining regimens of city life, but bound by a code of proper behavior and loyalty to friends, symbolized freedom and independence. The mountaineer had once been identified with such qualities, but by the end of the 1920s comic depictions of hillbillies or accounts of snake handling and other forms of eccentric behavior tarnished much of the romance associated with the mountains. Above all, persistent reports of Appalachian poverty and accounts of exploitation by coal operators and other economic interests significantly diminished the image of mountain independence. The cowboy, on the other hand, seemed peculiarly unmarked by negative stereotypes. In reality, he was basically a wageworker who was just as privy to exploitation as was the mountaineer. But in the world of popular imagination, where Americans encountered him most often, the cowboy remained a figure of unblemished virtue and assertive manhood. As a horseman, he commanded mobility and power, and stood as an irresistible symbol to workers and shopkeepers who possessed neither attribute.

The 1930s marked the heyday of cowboy music in the United States. Cowboy singers and bands could be heard on radio stations from Canada to the Mexican border and from New York to Los Angeles. Tin Pan Alley writers such as Billy Hill, Nick Kenny, Peter DeRose, and even Johnny Mercer poured out a steady stream of cowboy melodies, including one of the pop sensations of 1933, Billy Hill's "The Last Roundup." Lynn Riggs's Broadway production about cowboy life in Oklahoma, *Green Grow the Lilacs*, had only a short run after it was introduced in 1931, but it eventually became the basis of one of America's most famous musicals, *Oklahoma*.[33]

The embracing of western-style music in the 1930s was, in part, merely one facet of the larger retreat to popular culture—to gangster movies, Busby Berkeley musicals, big band jazz, radio serials—undertaken by Americans as a means of coping with hard times. The resurgence of interest in the cowboy, in both his musical and nonmusical guise, surely also must have its source in the renewed consciousness of and search for roots inspired by the Great Depression. In their search to regain a sense of purpose, many Americans may have found comfort in identifying with a reassuring symbol of independence and mastery, a collection of traits that the nation had once possessed and might once again assert. It is no wonder that word would go out of the White House that President Roosevelt's favorite song was "Home on the Range."

Although the cowboy entered the American consciousness through a variety of routes, no medium of popularization was more pervasive or influential than the Hollywood silver screen. And when the Mascot Company (a subsidiary of Republic Studios) signed Gene Autry to a contract in 1934, the myth of the singing cowboy simultaneously assumed a new dimension and gained the most potent forum yet for its widespread dissemination. Although long described as Oklahoma's "Singing Cowboy," Autry had a repertory, like most country entertainers of the era, that lacked clear definition. Songs like "Hillbilly Wedding in June," "A Gangster's Warning," and "High Behind Blues" appeared side by side in his repertory with such cowboy songs as "Empty Cot in the Bunk

House." His biggest hit, "Silver Haired Daddy of Mine," which was recorded as a duet with Jimmy Long in 1931, evoked a mountain image with its opening line: "In a vine-covered shack in the mountains." Nonwestern songs never disappeared from Autry's repertory, but after he moved to Hollywood, the cowboy persona took full control of his life and career. As Hollywood's singing cowboy he won a public exposure that far surpassed that of any other hillbilly singer—in the ninety movies he made between 1934 and 1954, in innumerable personal appearances including the famous rodeo at Madison Square Garden in New York, and on recordings and radio broadcasts.[34] People who heard or saw him easily made the equation that man with guitar equals cowboy singer. Although older cowboy actors and their fans may have been repelled by Autry's personality and boyish appearance, he became one of Hollywood's most popular and commercially successful personalities with a style that combined music, personal heroism, and Victorian morality. With his songs and Sears, Roebuck merchandised guitars, he did more than simply attract people to his performance and music; he also lent to that music the prestige and respectability of the American cowboy. Douglas B. Green's assessment of Autry's influence in country music bears close resemblance to that which Archie Green made of Bradley Kincaid. According to these scholars, both performers linked country music to satisfying images of respectability: Anglo-Saxonism and the cowboy myth. As Douglas Green noted, "no youngster in the thirties and forties ever wanted to grow up to be a hillbilly, but thousands upon thousands wanted to be cowboys, and by treating the country song with dignity and respect Autry made it part of the shining good deeds and character of the cowboy." [35]

As Autry's popularity mounted after 1934, membership in his band, or as part of his road show, provided an entrée for talented musicians who wanted access to both Hollywood and western music. Musicians joined his touring band as sidemen and appeared in his numerous movies and radio shows. Some were hillbilly performers who had earlier radio and recording experience—Smiley Burnette, Johnny Bond, Jimmy Wakely, Pat Buttram, the Cass County Boys. A few, like violinist Carl Cotner, were professional musicians who had little experience with country music. Autry also provided employment for such songwriters as Fred Rose and Cindy Walker, both of whom eventually became major influences in the country music business. Inspired by Autry's success, other Hollywood studios launched campaigns to find competitive singing cowboys. With few exceptions, most of Autry's competitors, such as Tex Ritter, Eddie Dean, Jimmy Wakely, Roy Rogers, Rex Allen, the Sons of the Pioneers, and the Riders of the Purple Sage, arrived in Hollywood as well-seasoned professional country musicians. Indeed, these actor/musicians constituted only a small fragment of the country musicians who have made the trek to Hollywood over the years to appear in films. Appearance in a movie or the signing of a movie contract became an event of prime importance for the country entertainer, an accomplishment that in many ways outranked the acquisition of a recording contract.

Autry was by no means the only inspiration, but "western" or "cowboy" entertainers enveloped the country music field in the 1930s. Surviving hillbilly music magazines, newspaper radio logs, and broadcasting magazines from the 1930s document the remarkable appeal exerted by western/cowboy symbolism. Cowboy singers and groups proliferated on radio broadcasts from Canada to the Mexican border, from New York City to California and in virtually every state in between, and even in far off Australia and New Zealand. Individual cowboy singers bearing names such as Red River Dave, Powder River Jack, the Yodeling Ranger, Cowboy Slim, the Lonesome Cowboy, Montana Slim, Patsy Montana, and the Texas Drifter vied with cowboy bands and singing groups who called themselves Radio Rangers, Radio Cowboys, Cowboy Ramblers, Westerners, Mountain Rangers, Drifting Pioneers, Trail Blazers, Range Riders, Riders of the Purple Sage, Sons of the Pioneers, Oklahoma Cowboys, Bar-X Cowboys, 101 Ranch Boys, Golden West Cowboys, Girls of the Golden West, Prairie Ramblers, and on and on. In the great rush to appropriate cowboy symbolism some musicians changed both their stage names and the focus of their music. The Kentucky Ramblers, for example, became the Prairie Ramblers and moved away from the hillbilly emphasis of their earlier years. In most cases, though, western names were adopted because of their romantic associations. When Dolly and Milly Good, farm girls from southern Illinois, began their careers as a close-harmony duet team in 1933, they had a wide-ranging repertory but no performing title. After naming them the Girls of the Golden West, their manager, Hank Richards, looked at a map of West Texas and discovered a small town with the colorful name of "Muleshoe." To the end of their professional career, the Good sisters were described not only as ranch girls from Muleshoe, Texas, but also as performers whose expert yodeling style had been influenced by the coyotes they heard howling on the windswept Texas Plains![36]

By the end of the 1930s the cowboy or western impulse had become a refuge for country entertainers, or their managers, who sought a respectable or more up-to-date alternative to the hillbilly image. Cowboy costuming was decidedly more romantic than any kind of clothing associated with rural plain folk life, and western-cut suits could in fact suggest the more dignified and hence more prosperous milieu of the rancher. Many of the cowboy songs, especially those from Tin Pan Alley, tended to be more sophisticated in style and structure than the typical hillbilly offerings. Country musicians who were receptive to hot dance or jazz instrumentation also gravitated toward the cowboy or western-style bands. The Sons of the Pioneers (originally composed of Bob Nolan from Canada, Tim Spencer from Missouri, and Roy Rogers from Ohio) won great fame as cowboy singers with a successful fusion of smooth harmonies, well-crafted romantic songs such as "Cool Water" and "Tumbling Tumbleweeds," and some of the best hot fiddling—by Texan Hugh Farr—heard anywhere in the 1930s.[37] Imitated by many western-oriented musical groups before World War II, this formula of polished singing and jazzlike instrumentation contributed strongly to a perception in both the public mind and among musicians that the music of the West was superior to that of the East.

If "cowboy" meant respectability for some country entertainers, "western" connoted "liberation" for others. Elements of truth do exist of course in the cowboy and western myths. The cultural and ethnic pluralism present in the western United States—with its mixture of Indian, Mexican, African, and Anglo elements—may have contributed to a similar diversity in musical styles, and the vastness of the western sky, and the grandeur of the region's landscapes, may have inspired a spirit of expansiveness that infused music and other cultural expressions. Nevertheless, it is important to note that the respective visions of cowboy and western life drew far more from popular culture and myth—from generations of dime novels, short-story magazines, cowboy songs, and Hollywood movies—than they did from reality. Country singers borrowed heavily from popular culture to fashion their versions of the cowboy myth, but then reinforced and recycled that myth through their music, performing attire, and life-styles. The cowboy/western mystique became the most popular alternative available to country musicians who felt limited by earlier forms of country music or who felt embarrassed by the rustic or hillbilly associations that clung to them. Hank Penny, for example, a singer and musician from Birmingham, Alabama, was certainly not alone in rejecting the country music that was native to his own region. Penny was contemptuous of the hillbilly music he heard on Nashville's "Grand Ole Opry." He named his own band the Radio Cowboys, appropriated music he associated with the Texas swing bands, and set out on a performing career that eventually carried him to professional success in California.[38]

In the mid 1930s, as Penny looked westward in his search for appealing musical alternatives, he found what he wanted in the styles of the "hot string bands" of Texas and Oklahoma. This was the genre of music that would eventually be described as Western Swing. Pioneer bands like the Light Crust Doughboys, the Musical Brownies, the Cowboy Ramblers, and the Texas Playboys created an exciting fusion of country, blues, pop, and jazz that they disseminated throughout the Southwest via radio broadcasts, recordings,[39] and innumerable personal appearances. The music could be appreciated in many formats, but its natural and most energizing habitat was the dance hall. In this setting thousands of people escaped from the anxieties of the Great Depression. Musicians, on the other hand, found employment, opportunities to engage in musical experimentation, and a respectable, but still grassroots, rival to hillbilly music. These were the driving forces that lured many innovative southeastern musicians, such as Merle Travis, Clifford Gross, Tex Atchison, Harold Hensley, and Hank Penny, into the performance of Western Swing.

The Southwest clearly provided an environment in which experimental styles of country music could be performed and appreciated. Powerful 50,000-watt radio stations; a few large cities like Dallas, Fort Worth, Houston, San Antonio, Tulsa, and New Orleans, where entertainment-hungry audiences abounded; an eclectic racial and ethnic mixture with exciting musical traditions (ranging from the Cajuns of southwestern Louisiana to the Mexicans of South Texas); a booming oil economy that provided some financial relief from the Depression; and a passion for dancing that crossed racial and ethnic lines, all contributed to the creation of a milieu ripe for Western Swing.[40]

The principal actors in this musical and social transformation were rural and small-town people, but the milieu in which they acted was a rapidly urbanizing one. Cowboys played only peripheral physical roles in the southwestern economy of the 1930s. But while his true function had become marginalized, the cowboy of romantic legend had taken center stage in the imaginations of musicians and promoters. The cowboy consequently became the centerpiece for the developing Western Swing genre. The career of Bob Wills best demonstrates the exploitation of the cowboy myth, and its use as a romantic dressing for a musical form that combined urban and rural motifs. Wills was the heir of old-time fiddlers on both sides of his family, and his own fiddle style remained close to those traditions throughout his life.[41] Wills, however, was also receptive to popular music, and he drew heavily on black blues forms and small-band jazz. Although he spent sixteen years of his life in the ranching country of West Texas (near Memphis), from the age of eight until he moved to Fort Worth at twenty-four, cowboys played no apparent role in the formation of his musical taste or style. Wills had fiddled often for ranch dances,[42] but these affairs seem to have differed little from the house dances of East Texas and the southern United States. His move to Fort Worth in 1929 was the central event of the young musician's life, because it placed him more directly in contact with the urban musical styles and methods of dissemination that most strongly appealed to him. Contrary to the interpretation presented by Wills's principal biographer, who strove to connect the man and his music to the liberating environment of the West,[43] Wills was instead a child of popular culture. His music

came neither from cowboys nor from blacks with whom he had
worked in the cotton fields of West Texas; his eclectic mixture of
sounds came from phonograph recordings, radio broadcasts, and
the larger spectrum of commercial American music.
When Wills organized his Texas Playboys in 1933, the band
name he chose and the musical repertory he favored indicated the
urbane and eclectic bent of this Texas country boy. His fiddle style
revealed debts to both the rural music of his southern forebears
and to the black blues that had seductively captivated him. Wills
bitterly resisted the label "hillbilly," however, and he set out to
create a style of string band music that would appeal both to rural
and urban people while avoiding what he considered the rube
connotations of country music. The urban impulse and manipu-
lation of the Playboy title and image, though, did not prevent
Wills's eventual acceptance of the "western" label to describe his
music. The term "Western Swing" actually did not gain currency
until about 1946 when it was used to describe the music of Spade
Cooley in California. Wills and his musicians began their own
transition to a western identity in 1940 when they made their
first movie in California. Wills eventually appeared in fifteen
movies, performing a few songs and playing supportive roles to
such cowboy actors as Charles Starrett and Johnny Mack Brown.
Cowboy-style songs written for these movies began to appear in
the Playboys' repertory for the first time, and at least a couple of
them, "Dusty Skies" and "Cherokee Maiden," became commercial hits. The Playboys' musical style, however, did not change
substantially in the post-Hollywood years. The most dramatic
change came in their stage attire. The Playboys now appeared in
conservative western-style clothing, and Wills stood before them
in white cowboy hat projecting the aura of a prosperous and con-
fident rancher. The true cowboys of the West had exerted little
influence on the music of Western Swing, but the cowboys of

popular culture—the heroes of the silver screen—permanently marked the way that music was to be publicly perceived.

Country musicians at the beginning of World War II still strongly displayed the temptation or need to play cowboy, mountaineer, or some other role. But the cowboy persona clearly dominated the country music scene. Musicians everywhere wore cowboy or western-cut costumes, gave themselves cowboy stage names, or otherwise identified with western or ranch-style motifs. Well after the war was over, when country music had become a major force in American commercial entertainment, the compulsion to play cowboy or to package the music in cowboy symbolism remained strong. When Columbia Records issued its first budget album of the music of Roy Acuff, the mountain boy from East Tennessee who had dominated the country field during the war years, the company enclosed the record in a jacket depicting a cowboy sitting on his horse and gazing at a large black bird outlined against a romantic western landscape![44] The great country superstar of the early 1950s, Hank Williams, who had grown up in rural Alabama as the son of a log train operator, felt moved to call himself the Drifting Cowboy. One of his chief rivals, Nova Scotia–born Hank Snow, called himself the Singing Ranger and regularly dressed in the gaudiest "cowboy style" costumes available. Williams and Snow were only two examples of a rather universal tendency in country music to mask the performer's true identity under a romantic western stage name or in an ersatz cowboy costume. The cowboy had won the day in country music.

Even though the cowboy apparently corralled country music, the lure of the mountains had not died. Some musicians who came from the Appalachians, or who identified with that region, competed favorably with the host of entertainers from Texas who dominated the jukeboxes during the war. It was difficult, however, to distinguish a "mountain sound" from any other kind of old-time

rural music, and no stage costume defined or encapsulated mountain life. For male entertainers, hillbilly garb served only comic
purposes, but for women country performers, long, old-fashioned
dresses, particularly on the more tradition-oriented shows such as
the "Renfro Valley Barn Dance," played dual roles. Such costumes
could, like those of their male counterparts, recall the world of
Mammy Yokum, or they could evoke the spirit, not simply of the
Appalachian South, but of all rural America. In the absence of
defining costumes, or of sounds that truly echoed Appalachian
culture, mountain musicians had no recourse but to exploit evoca-
tive place names or certain impulses that fulfilled popular stereotypes about mountain culture. Hence, one finds a continued usage
down through the 1950s of band names like Smoky Mountain
Boys, Tennessee Mountain Boys, Clinch Mountain Boys, Clinch
Mountain Clan, Foggy Mountain Boys, Cumberland Mountain
Folk, and Confederate Mountaineers. Songs commemorating the
old mountain home, or expressing a longing for it, still appeared
in country music, and a few of them—such as "Foggy Mountain
Breakdown," "Country Roads" (about West Virginia), "Smoky
Mountain Memories," and "Rocky Top, Tennessee"—achieved
immense popularity. Country audiences still exhibited periodically a symbolic need to go back home, and that home was often
in the mountains.

Mood may have been a central ingredient in the success enjoyed
by Roy Acuff during the war years. This self-styled Smoky Mountain Boy from near Knoxville, Tennessee,[45] made himself virtually
the symbol of American country music around the world. Acuff
was a compelling singer whose passionate sincerity and tearful
voice commanded the attention of listeners, but the overall mood
and symbolism associated with his music may have made him
doubly appealing in a period of social dislocation when people
thought of home and the traditional values it represented. Acuff's

music was "rural" rather than "mountain," but when he lifted his voice in the mournful cadences of "way back in the hills when a boy I once wandered,"[46] he may have transported millions of listeners back to a symbolic source of American culture itself, the hills of home.

Roy Acuff's commercial ascendancy during the 1940s really marked the last hurrah for the mountain style in mainstream country music. Appalachian-born musicians continued to appear with considerable frequency, and while some of them, such as Molly O'Day, Wilma Lee Cooper, the Bailes Brothers, Jimmy Dickens, the Louvin Brothers, Loretta Lynn, Dolly Parton, Mel Street, Keith Whitley, and Ricky Skaggs, have preserved many traditional elements and songs, most of the mountain-derived musicians have been little different from other country entertainers. The majority of modern mountain musicians have looked elsewhere, in fact, for stylistic and commercial inspiration. Loretta Lynn, who promoted herself as the "coal miner's daughter," was born in the Kentucky mountains, but she looked toward Ernest Tubb, the Texas honky tonk singer, as her commercial mentor in the early days of her career. Virginia's Mel Street and Kentucky's Keith Whitley similarly created their singing styles out of models provided by Texas honky tonk singers such as George Jones and Lefty Frizzell. Chet Atkins, from the Tennessee hills, looked beyond country music to the worlds of popular music and jazz to fashion his progressive style of guitar playing.[47] Nevertheless, country music industry publicists, fans, and the entertainers themselves still find commercial utility in the exploitation of images associated with mountain life. We are regularly reminded of Loretta Lynn's and Dolly Parton's "mountain freshness" or of the "Appalachian purity" heard in the singing of Lynn, Parton, or Skaggs. On her television shows Dolly Parton frequently chose physical settings such as her grandfather's church, the old homeplace, and family reunions to remind viewers not only of her mountain roots but also of the wholesomeness associated with that way of life. When Ricky Skaggs made his ascent to commercial fame in the early 1980s, as the first of country music's neotraditionalists, reviews and publicity accounts often associated his sound and clear tenor with his origins in the Kentucky mountains. As he resurrected older songs, Skaggs did more than simply revive a sense of tradition in country music. He also reinforced the feeling that mountain life and mountain music represented traditional morality and a way of calling country music back to its better self—a feeling first conveyed nearly sixty years earlier by Bradley Kincaid, reasserted in Roy Acuff's wartime performances, and echoed once again in Dolly Parton's television shows.

Ricky Skaggs came to mainstream country music with the sensibilities of a musician who had sung and played bluegrass for most of his life. And bluegrass claimed country music's strongest surviving link to the Appalachians. The bluegrass style took shape in the years immediately following World War II when Bill Monroe, a singer and mandolin player from Rosine, Kentucky, created a dynamic, blues-based form of string band music that was punctuated by Monroe's own high-pitched style of singing.[48] Monroe and his popular band, the Blue Grass Boys (named after his home state of Kentucky), took their brand of music to the Grand Ole Opry in Nashville, and therefore made it easily accessible to other performers through the powerful broadcasts of WSM, Opry road shows, and phonograph recordings. By the middle of the 1950s a burgeoning list of musicians who had once played with Monroe or who had been inspired by his music had created a style of music which was being described as "bluegrass." Bluegrass music, by the end of that decade, had moved well beyond its original base in the small towns and hamlets of the South. Energized above all by the sensational three-finger banjo style of Earl Scruggs, the music reached a national audience through its discovery and promotion by the urban folk revival. Revolutionary in sound, yet traditional in its adherence to acoustic instrumentation and the use of old-time songs and singing, bluegrass became a refuge for country fans and musicians who looked with despair at the homogenization of mainstream country music. In the minds of many people, bluegrass became the logical extension or modern embodiment of mountain music. The music's presumed association with mountain culture contributed strongly to its embrace by the folk revival in the 1960s; the revival in turn sparked an even stronger affirmation of bluegrass's alleged mountain roots as a new generation of fans, collectors, and scholars—many of whom were musicians—became attracted to the style.

Bluegrass of course does have important ties to mountain culture, and to musicians with mountain origins. Robert Cantwell, whose brilliant study *Bluegrass Breakdown* is the most provocative interpretation yet written on any field of country music, has in fact ventured the observation that "bluegrass was and is the music of the Appalachian people."[49] As Cantwell and others have recognized, a large number of bluegrass entertainers, including such seminal figures as Earl Scruggs, Lester Flatt, Jimmy Martin, the Osborne Brothers (Sonny and Bob), the McReynolds Brothers (Jim and Jesse), and the Stanley Brothers (Carter and Ralph) hailed from the southeastern hill country. In the formative years of the genre, bluegrass musicians often resurrected songs that had been identified with older mountain performers; the Stanley Brothers, for example, with their recorded versions of such songs as "Little Maggie," "Handsome Molly," and "Maple On the Hill," borrowed extensively from the repertories of groups like Grayson and Whitter and Mainer's Mountaineers. The Stanley Brothers, who came from Virginia's Clinch Mountains, lived long enough to see their own songs borrowed by the next generation of bluegrass musicians. The Stanleys' contemporaries, Lester Flatt and Earl Scruggs, made the most explicit connection between bluegrass and mountain music when they recorded a superb tribute to the Carter Family, a recording composed exclusively of the Family's songs and which featured the autoharp playing of Maybelle Carter.[50]

Bluegrass has also had a passionate following in Appalachia and among many Appalachian people who have moved elsewhere. Flatt and Scruggs, for instance, took their brand of bluegrass to Carnegie Hall and college campuses all over the United States, but they also played constantly in little communities all over the hill country that were scarcely large enough for a post office. Bluegrass also exhibited great strength in Baltimore; Washington, D.C.; Cincinnati, Dayton, and Akron, Ohio; Detroit; and in other cities where southeastern migrants congregated.

Although specific ties between bluegrass and earlier Appalachian musical expressions do exist, the connections should not be exaggerated. Some of the music's most influential personalities, including Bill Monroe, came from areas well outside the mountains. Monroe grew up in western Kentucky in a county bordering the Ohio River, while Chubby Wise, the music's first seminal fiddler, came from Florida. The blues tradition, which deeply inspired these two musicians, shaped the bluegrass sound as much as did any other source. The bluegrass musicians built their repertories out of the varied materials of America's musical past. In describing the music of the Monroe Brothers, the duet composed of Bill and his brother Charlie who recorded sixty numbers for Victor from 1936 to 1938, Robert Cantwell asserted that they had presented "a stylized picture of the Appalachian region."[51] More precisely, with a catalogue of songs dealing with such rustic pastimes and institutions as rabbit hunts, watermelons hanging on the vine, new river trains, country churches, and weeping

willows, the Monroe Brothers had instead painted a musical por-
trait of the *rural* South. Like other fans and writers who have
been drawn irresistibly to the enduring romance of the southern
mountains, Robert Cantwell heard the Monroe Brothers present
a songbag that was generically rural, and translated it into something specifically Appalachian. The most interesting linkage between bluegrass and mountain culture lies therefore in the area
of symbolism—the way the musicians see themselves, but above
all in the way that outsiders perceive them and their music. Like
all forms of music, bluegrass fragmented into a variety of substyles
as it became popular and reached out to a growing number of
fans and musicians; its evolution consequently has inspired an-
guished debates about purity and identity. Nevertheless, a very
large contingent of bluegrass musicians and fans have always insisted that their music is not only purer than other forms of country music (i.e., less tainted by commercialism, and more strongly
rooted in tradition), but that it is also more moral than those
styles which emanate from Nashville. Mercifully, no one speaks of
"Anglo-Saxon" roots any longer, but a disquieting attribution of
"celticism,"[52] which ignores bluegrass's multicultural sources, has
crept into discussions of the music's style and origins. As in the
days of Bradley Kincaid, visions of musical, cultural, and ethnic
purity have been revived to distinguish a form of country music
from its presumably inferior and more commercial competitors.
And, once again, the southern mountains and its music become
benchmarks to remind country music of both its "sources" and its
"heresies."

While the mountain impulse was being reasserted through the
medium of bluegrass, it was winning even larger circulation
through the forum of the folk revival.[53] Mountain singers of course
had been fueling and sustaining earlier versions of the revival
since the 1930s when Aunt Molly Jackson and Jim Garland took

their protest songs from Kentucky to New York City. The audiences who heard them and later Appalachian stylists such as Texas Gladden and Jean Ritchie, however, were miniscule compared to the massive following won by the revival singers of the 1960s. Once the later revival got underway—ironically, with the Kingston Trio's watered-down version of a North Carolina murder ballad, "Tom Dooley"—many fans and musicians began looking beyond the pop-style folk songs that dominated the music charts hoping to find the authentic roots of America's folk music. This quest led many revivalists back to the southern hills—in a search for singers and musicians who preserved the old-time songs and styles, to festivals where traditional music was emphasized, to phonograph recordings of early hillbilly performers, and to modern commercial forms, such as bluegrass, which seemed to be keeping the flame of Appalachian music alive.

Like the folk collectors of the pre–World War I period, those folk revivalists who came South in the 1960s spent most of their time in the southeastern hill country; very few ventured into the Southwest. It was not simply an Appalachian fixation that lured them to the Southeast; young collectors and musicians took advantage of the proximity of the hills to the large eastern population centers, and to the eastern universities where folk music interest was strong. Folk festivals had been a part of southeastern life since 1928, but the venerable fiddlers' contest at Union Grove, North Carolina, and the festival at Galax, Virginia, emerged as immense "happenings" in the 1960s, when they were discovered first by the folk revival community, and later by members of the counterculture who began making them part of their back-to-nature movement.

One of the happiest consequences of the folk revival's excursion into old-time music was the rediscovery of such surviving mountain singers from early commercial hillbilly music as Dock Boggs,

Clarence Ashley, and Buell Kazee.[54] And as these men renewed their careers at folk festivals and before university audiences, a new group of mountain-born musicians, including Tommy Jarrell, Hazel Dickens and Arthel "Doc" Watson, were introduced to revival audiences. For many of the young revivalists who ventured into the hills in the 1960s, their love affairs with the music of the mountains served as transforming events that permanently changed their lives. Ralph Rinzler, John Cohen, Tom Paley, Alice Foster, Alan Jabbour, Richard Blaustein, and Mike Seeger numbered among the many northern-born and city-bred musicians whose lives became consumed with mountain lore and mountain music. They expended most of their energies collecting songs, listening to old records, writing album notes and magazine articles, interviewing, recording, and filming musicians, booking concerts for various performers, and learning to play the old-time styles that they heard. Cohen, Seeger, and Paley organized a string band called the New Lost City Ramblers and set out to recreate faithfully the songs and styles of early commercial hillbilly music. Although the musicians from whom they borrowed represented a wide variety of regions in the South, the Ramblers could not resist lending a mountain cast to the music they performed. Their first album included four songs taken from recordings by Uncle Dave Macon and the McGee Brothers, who hailed from central Tennessee; Cliff Carlisle, who came from Louisville, Kentucky; and the Dallas String Band, a black band from Texas. Nevertheless, the record liner notes alleged that "the songs on this album were recorded by commercial companies and the Library of Congress in the southeastern mountains between 1925 and 1935." Despite the inclusion of items like "Battleship of Maine" that referred to relatively recent events, as well as others like "Dallas Rag," "Tom Cat Blues," "Brown's Ferry Blues," and "Take A Drink On Me" that clearly suggested early-twentieth-century commercial derivation, the notes insisted that the album's songs were "old traditional songs that had been in the mountains since pioneer days."[55] Through many recordings, concerts, and a popular songbook, the Ramblers inspired a host of similar "revivalist" bands, such as the Red Clay Ramblers, the Highwoods String Band, and the Hot Mud Family, who still command the allegiances of thousands of fans.[56]

As we have seen, the folk revivalists of the 1960s were interested, almost exclusively, in the music of the Southeast, in either its mountain guise or as bluegrass. Even when they utilized the music of performers who came from areas far outside the Appalachians, the revivalists seemed unable to resist the temptation to subsume such music under the "mountain" rubric. The New Lost City Ramblers' Appalachian fixation has been noted earlier, but similar tendencies remain apparent today in the work of many people, both academic and free-lance, who promote or write about old-time music. A reviewer of Doc Watson's album *My Dear Old Southern Home*, for example, described its contents as "songs of the traditional country music of Appalachia," even though the collection included songs learned from Jimmie Rodgers, Gene Autry, and the nineteenth-century composer Henry Clay Work. The respected folklorist Norm Cohen, who is an alumnus of the folk revival, was similarly casual in his references to the mountains in the notes to his invaluable *Minstrels and Tunesmiths* collection. He rightly asserted the centrality of nineteenth-century pop music as a source of early country music, but he then clouded the identity of the latter form of music by referring to the presence of recording devices, pianos, and sheet music in "southern mountain homes" early in this century.[57] Through the musicians they favored or promoted, the record liner notes and articles they wrote, and the music they performed, the revivalists reshaped and revitalized the concept of mountain music. In doing so, they reaffirmed the idea that such music was the core and soul of country music, and a way to measure the extent to which country music had strayed from its original sound and mission.

Despite their passionate commitment to folk music and folk culture, the revivalists paid little attention to surviving cowboy music traditions and still less to Western Swing and other southwestern styles. Revivalist string bands were much more likely to favor and record the music of Georgian Gid Tanner or North Carolinian Charlie Poole than that of Texans Milton Brown or Bob Wills. Some Texas fiddle music was reissued on record anthologies, and a few Texas musicians, like fiddler Eck Robertson and cowboy singer Carl Sprague, were interviewed or otherwise reintroduced to festival audiences.[58] When the revival of interest in southwestern and cowboy music began in the early 1970s, the awakening came largely through the efforts of country music insiders—collectors and musicians. Western Swing, for example, had been preserved to some extent in the music of such professional country entertainers as Hank Thompson, Ray Price, Red Steagall, Hoyle Nix, Willie Nelson, and Merle Haggard, who had maintained a reverence for the music they had grown up with, that of Bob Wills and the Texas Playboys.[59] The most self-conscious efforts at revivalism, however, came in the music of younger entertainers such as fiddler Alvin Crow or the members of a band called Asleep at the Wheel. Making their headquarters in Austin, Texas, during the mid 1970s when that city gained fame as an active and energetic music center, these musicians built successful commercial styles for themselves while reintroducing such veteran Western Swing performers as Jesse Ashlock, Floyd Tillman, J. R. Chatwell, and Cliff Bruner to enthusiastic audiences. The renewed interest in Western Swing encouraged many of the older musicians to return to professional music. Largely through the patronage of Merle Haggard, a modern version of the Texas

Playboys led by steel guitarist Leon McAuliffe once again became active and won passionate support from both older and younger fans. Illness prevented Bob Wills from resuming his career, but before his death in 1975 he had already become virtually a cult figure among many musicians and fans who saw him as either the greatest innovator in country music history or as a liberated musician who had completely transcended the country music idiom.[60]

Country entertainers, of course, had never lost their fascination with the cowboy. Country stage costuming is only the most obvious example of exploitation of the cowboy or western image. No one any longer wears the gaudy, bespangled, and brightly colored Nudie suits that dominated stage attire through the 1960s, but boots and cowboy hats are still quite common among both bluegrass and mainstream country performers, and are particularly noticeable among the neotraditionalists, such as George Strait, Garth Brooks, and Alan Jackson, in the 1990s (such performers are in fact often described as "hat acts"). Songs dealing with cowboys, ersatz and real, or which use the cowboy as a metaphor for some contemporary concern, still appear frequently in country music. Something approaching a mini-renaissance of traditional-style cowboy songs began in the 1980s when singer and scholar Douglas B. Green, calling himself "Ranger Doug," and dressing like a movie cowboy of the 1940s, founded a trio with Fred LaBour and Woody Paul called "Riders in the Sky." Combining humor, clever stage sets that included bleached cow skulls and tumbleweeds, trick roping, romantic cowboy songs, hot fiddling, yodeling (expertly done by Ranger Doug), and smooth harmonies, the trio imaginatively concocted a modern fantasy of a musical world that was never anything more than a fantasy itself. Modern songs that consciously re-create the sound and ambience of the movies' singing cowboys seldom become big commercial successes, nor do the traditional cowboy songs that are occasionally revived by such singers as Chris LeDoux, Glenn Ohrlin, Ian Tyson, Michael Martin Murphey, Red Steagall, or Don Edwards. Nevertheless, their periodic reappearances provide constant reminders of the enduring appeal of the cowboy.[61]

The cowboy has indeed remained central to the self-identification of country musicians and their fans, but the cowboys of modern country music, as represented by both musicians and singers, no longer inhabit the Old West but instead embody current preoccupations and fantasies. In the 1970s, for example, the cowboy became emblematic of a host of counterestablishment alternatives—some of which ran counter to each other. A small coterie of mainstream country musicians, including Waylon Jennings, Willie Nelson, and Tompall Glaser, became identified as "rebels" in Nashville when they flaunted hedonistic life-styles and experimented with rock and other "unapproved" musical forms. As is often true of cultural "rebellions," this particular one proved to be commercially profitable, at least for Jennings and Nelson, who found that a great deal of money could be made by "standing up" against the Nashville establishment. Jennings remained anchored to Nashville and to the powerful RCA Corporation for which he recorded, while Nelson relocated in Austin in 1972. Both entertainers, however, soon became the nucleus of a group of free-spirited musicians, including Jerry Jeff Walker, who were known as the "Austin Outlaws." Jennings went through a phase of sporting a beard and dressing ominously in black cowboy clothing, a new persona that was well summed up by the title of one of his recordings from that period, *Ladies Love Outlaws.* [62] Nelson, on the other hand, entered a period of eclectic life-style experimentation, ranging from hippie attire to Indian costuming, before settling in on the dress and demeanor of a rough-hewn cowpoke.

As Nelson moved from the mainstream of Nashville country music to the fringe of the counterculture, he encountered and became the cultural godfather of a group of young musicians in Austin who were moving from the fringe toward the country music center. The Austin musicians, and their fans, experimented with drugs and free life-styles, and exhibited an affinity not only for the music of Texas but also for the music being produced by their youthful contemporaries in other parts of the nation. As the centripetal force of country music pulled them inward, they sought and found cultural mentors in people like Nelson, Floyd Tillman, Jesse Ashlock (a former Texas Playboy fiddler), and Kenneth Threadgill, the singing-proprietor of an Austin honky tonk. They also appropriated clothing and symbols—like long-horn steers, longneck beers, and armadillos—that would legiti-mate their music and cater to the tastes of people in central Texas and the surrounding hill country. In so doing, they also dis-tinguished themselves from most rock musicians elsewhere. Like Gram Parsons's and Chris Hillman's experimental and influential country-rock band from California, the Flying Burrito Brothers, the young Austin musicians seized upon the cowboy as the most usable symbol to define and embody the free-spirited musical cul-ture that they were busily building. The spectacle of quasi-hippies dressing like cowboys and performing a musical fusion of country, rock, and Western Swing seemed so novel that both participants and observers were hard-pressed to find an appropriate descriptive label for the music. Some critics favored "redneck rock," but when Michael Murphey wrote and recorded "Cosmic Cowboy," he may have come closest to capturing the sense of absurdity involved in the marriage of countercultural values and country music.[63]

It is clear, then, that the reassertion of the cowboy image since the 1970s represents much more than a search by musicians for alternative forms of musical expression. The cowboy has been called into action repeatedly to represent a variety of life-styles that are satisfying to both entertainers and fans. The oldest of such impulses, and one which has run deeply in country music history since at least the days of Jimmie Rodgers, is represented in the careers of musicians like Johnny Cash, Willie Nelson, Waylon Jennings, Charlie Daniels, and Hank Williams, Jr. When these entertainers dress in cowboy attire and assume a swaggering "badman" posture, they are playing out the ancient tradition of the "rambling man." Identification with the hedonistic rambler, whether in the guise of the gambler, the rounder, the outlaw, the drifter, the hobo, or the footloose lover, has been an essentially harmless form of fantasizing for both the entertainer and his fans. The rambler theme, it is true, can assume a bittersweet poignance in such rodeo songs as Ian Tyson's "Some Day Soon" or George Strait's "Amarillo By Morning," which document the strains in human relationships often wrought by nomadic occupations or life-styles. But in the music of men like Charlie Daniels and Hank Williams, Jr., an exaggerated pose of machismo sometimes bares an overtly political stance of jingoism and nativism. Whether calling for vigilante action against alleged drug kingpins or threatening violent retribution against Saddam Hussein, the songs of such musicians suggest a virtually impassable gulf between country music's modern outlaw cowboys and the benign singing cowboys of the 1930s.

It is true that the roles played by country musicians usually convey meanings no deeper than the simple desire to entertain, and that their varying stage personas embody nothing more than innocent fantasies. But as we have seen in the careers of individuals like Bradley Kincaid, Gene Autry, Bob Wills, and Jean Ritchie, stage roles can also be cultural statements because they tie certain forms of public entertainment to ways of life that are deemed to be culturally superior. Such identification simultaneously lends legitimacy and respectability to certain forms of music and to the cultures they represent. The entertainer reaches past his own immediate circumstances, and those of his listeners, to suggest a culture and way of life that are more exciting or valid than those of the present. Assumed stage identities therefore sometimes either reflect or inspire deep-seated cultural longings or insecurities in both the entertainer and his audience. Country musicians, after all, have usually been neither mountaineers nor cowboys. They and their core audience have been instead working people—farmers, mill operatives, mechanics, coal miners, oil workers, truck drivers, sales clerks, cooks, waitresses, beauticians—whose roots and value systems lie, preponderantly, in the fundamentalist rural South. The commercialization of their music, a phenomenon whose contours took shape most dramatically in the decades since 1920, has been but the most recent manifestation of well over a century of revolutionary, though gradual, social transformation in residence, occupation, and life-style. Whether welcomed or not—and nothing compels us to believe that the southern folk really resisted the opportunities to improve their material conditions—the changes that marked the transition to urban-industrial life have been far from painless; they have often been accompanied by frustration, disappointment, alienation, and a sense of loss. Locked too often in dead-end jobs that offer neither fulfillment nor security, and living in an American society that values neither working people nor work unless glamorous or status related, southern working folk often don cultural clothing that reaffirms their identity, provides bonding with people like themselves, or reestablishes continuity with an older way of life. As one of many available cultural responses, country music has offered escape and catharsis from present realities, while also providing self-affirmation through such security-laden symbols as home, family, church, and the South.[64] The mountaineer and the mountains are sometimes resurrected in songs and popular culture (as witnessed by the remarkable success of the 1970s television series "The Waltons") to revive the sense of rustic virtue, domestic warmth, and tradition that seem absent from modern urban life. The cowboy and the West, however, have been the most recurring and powerful of available symbols, in part because they are concepts of immense plasticity which offer to musician and audience alike a wide range of imaginative possibilities. The symbols therefore can evoke innocent visions of escape, or they can be tinted by the political coloration of the times in which they exist, or they can be a combination of both. Images of a limitless Western landscape dominated by the Man on Horseback can inspire campaigns for both personal and national renewal, or they can mask deep-seated desires for reassertions of masculine dominance, flight from responsibility, and easy solutions to complex problems.

Country musicians and songwriters of course no longer speak exclusively for themselves or for a limited constituency of transplanted rural Southerners. Country music has moved well beyond its original regional parameters as it has become a major voice of lower- and middle-class people throughout America. Indeed, as the urban cowboy phenomenon of the early 1980s suggested, the music sometimes strikes a responsive chord in the hearts of people who have neither southern nor working-class origins. The western myth would have died long ago had it not found resonance in the hearts and minds of a large segment of the American people everywhere. The cowboy will retain his appeal as long as Americans identify with the kind of freedom that he supposedly represents, or as long as they cling to the illusion of their country's preindustrial virtue and innocence. Many Americans will always find succor in "the deep rolling hills of old Virginia," or in other romantic mountain settings; an increasing number of country performers are in fact finding Branson, Missouri, in the Ozarks to be the ideal locale to showcase their talent. Although a large segment of the American public would indeed like to escape to "Rocky Top, Tennessee" beyond the reach of "smoggy smoke" and "telephone bills," the majority of country performers and fans still find their spiritual and aesthetic salvation in the West, in places like the mythical hamlet of "Luckenbach, Texas" with "Willie, Waylon, and the boys." And while they would have to be as wealthy as a major recording star to pull it off, many probably agree with Merle Haggard in wishing a release, and to have the independence to demand of the world that it "turn me loose, set me free, somewhere in the middle of Montana."[65]

Notes

One. Southern Rural Music in the Nineteenth Century

1. Bill C. Malone, *Country Music, USA*, rev. ed. (Austin: University of Texas Press, 1985; orig. pub., 1968); "Hillbilly Issue," *Journal of American Folklore*, 78 (July–September 1965).

2. The concept of "country dance" won popularity in Great Britain and the American colonies largely through the successive publications of John Playford's seminal *The English Dancing Master* beginning in 1651. Known in its many later editions and supplements as *The Dancing Master*, the book inspired an enthusiasm for dances of presumed country origin among the upper classes on both sides of the English Channel.

3. For a short discussion of Cal Stewart's career, as well as a recorded example of his style, see Norm Cohen, ed., *Minstrels and Tunesmiths: The Commercial Roots of Early Country Music* (John Edwards Memorial

Foundation JEMF 109). The Toby character is discussed in Larry Clark, "Toby Shows: a Form of American Popular Theater," Ph.D. dissertation, University of Illinois, 1963; Sherwood Snyder III, "The Toby Shows," Ph.D. dissertation, University of Minnesota, 1966; Neil E. Schaffner, with Vance Johnson, *The Fabulous Toby and Me* (Englewood Cliffs, N.J.: Prentice-Hall, 1968); and William Lawrence Slout, *Theatre in a Tent* (Bowling Green, Ohio: Bowling Green State University Popular Press, 1972).

4. Neither published nor recorded anthologies of such songs exist, but see Nicholas E. Tawa, *A Music for the Millions: Antebellum Democratic Attitudes and the Birth of American Popular Music* (New York: Pendragon Press, 1984), 4–6, 34, 38–39, 42–43. For somewhat comparable attitudes in England, see Jan Marsh, *Back to the Land: The Pastoral Impulse in England from 1880 to 1914* (London: Quartet Books, 1982), especially "Folk Song Restored," 72–89.

5. Bill C. Malone, *Southern Music/American Music* (Lexington: University Press of Kentucky, 1979); Earl F. Bargainneer, "Tin Pan Alley and Dixie: The South in Popular Song," *Mississippi Quarterly*, 30 (Fall 1977), 527–575; Theodore Wallace Johnson, "Black Images in American Popular Song, 1840–1910," Ph.D. dissertation, Northwestern University, 1975.

6. John A. Lomax, *Cowboy Songs and Other Frontier Ballads* (New York: Sturgis & Walton, 1910); Olive Dame Campbell and Cecil J. Sharp, *English Folk Songs from the Southern Appalachians* (New York: Putnam's, 1917).

7. Lawrence Levine, *Black Culture and Black Consciousness: Afro-American Folk Thought from Slavery to Freedom* (New York: Oxford University Press, 1977), 24.

8. For differing interpretations concerning southern music's distinctiveness, see Grady McWhiney, *Cracker Culture: Celtic Ways in the Old South* (Tuscaloosa: University of Alabama Press, 1988); Norm Cohen, review of Bill C. Malone, *Southern Music/American Music*, in *Western Folklore*, 4 (October 1981), 348–350; Robert Shelton, *The Country Music Story* (New York: Bobbs-Merrill, 1966); Dickson Bruce, Jr., *And*

They All Sang Hallelujah: Plain-Folk Camp Meeting Religion, 1800–1845 (Knoxville: University of Tennessee Press, 1974); and Alan Lomax, *The Folk Songs of North America* (Garden City, N.Y.: Doubleday, 1960).

9. McWhiney, *Cracker Culture*, 113–123.

10. David Hackett Fischer, *Albion's Seed* (New York: Oxford University Press, 1989), 313–314, 621, 672.

11. Carl Bridenbaugh, *Vexed and Troubled Englishmen, 1590–1642* (New York: Oxford University Press, 1968), 21.

12. Fischer, *Albion's Seed*, 621.

13. Carl Bridenbaugh, *Myths and Realities: Societies of the Colonial South* (New York: Atheneum, 1963), 131, 132.

14. Samuel Bayard, *Hill Country Tunes; Instrumental Folk Music of Southwestern Pennsylvania* (Philadelphia. American Folklore Society, 1944), xii, xxv–xxvi. Don Yoder, *Pennsylvania Spirituals* (Lancaster: Pennsylvania Folklife Society, 1961), viii.

15. Yoder, 8, 9.

16. S. Foster Damon, "History of Square Dancing," American Antiquarian Society, *Proceedings* (April 1952), 63–98.

17. Barry Ancelet, *Cajun Music: Its Origin and Development* (Lafayette: Center for Louisiana Studies, University of Southwestern Louisiana, 1989), 17.

18. Manuel Pena has written the best account of Conjunto music, *The Texas-Mexican Conjunto: History of a Working-Class Music* (Austin: University of Texas Press, 1985). Pena, however, argues that German influence was exerted in Mexico before acculturation occurred in Texas (see pp. 35–36).

19. George Pullen Jackson, *White Spirituals in the Southern Uplands* (Chapel Hill: University of North Carolina Press, 1933; reprint, 1965), 31–34. See also Harry Eskew, "Shape-Note Hymnody in the Shenandoah Valley, 1816–1860," Ph.D. dissertation, Tulane University, 1966.

20. Cohen, Review of Malone, *Southern Music/American Music*, 350.

21. Recorded examples of such music include *Altamont: Black Stringband Music from the Library of Congress* (Rounder 0238), and *String Bands, 1927–1929* (HK Records 4009). Published narratives from the

WPA collection may be found in George P. Rawick, ed., *The American Slave: A Composite Autobiography*, 19 vols., 22 supps. (Westport, Conn.: Greenwood Press, 1972–1979).

22. T. H. Breen and Stephen Innes, *"Myne Owne Ground": Race and Freedom on Virginia's Eastern Shore, 1640–1676* (New York: Oxford University Press, 1980), 35, 59, 104–107; Alan Kulikoff, *Tobacco and Slaves: The Development of Southern Culture in the Chesapeake, 1680–1800* (Chapel Hill: University of North Carolina Press, 1986), esp. chap. 8; Mechal Sobel, *The World They Made Together: Black and White Values in Eighteenth-Century Virginia* (Princeton, N.J.: Princeton University Press, 1987).

23. See John Boles, *Religion in Antebellum Kentucky* (Lexington: University Press of Kentucky, 1976); and Boles, ed., *Masters and Slaves in the House of the Lord: Race and Religion in the American South, 1740–1870* (Lexington: University Press of Kentucky, 1988).

24. The best overall survey of black music in America is Eileen Southern, *The Music of Black Americans: A History* (New York: Norton, 1971).

25. A wide range of Civil War material has been consulted for this essay, but the most useful source has been a journal that concentrated on the reminiscences and memoirs of ex-Southern soldiers: *Confederate Veteran*. I examined issues published from 1893 through 1914.

26. I examined many of these songbooks in the Harris Collection, John Hay Library, Brown University. Included were such items as *Stonewall Song Book* (Richmond: West & Johnson, 1864), *The General Lee Songster* (Augusta, Ga.: John C. Schreiber & Son, 1865), *The Beauregard Songster* (Macon & Savannah, Ga.: John C. Schreiber, 1864), *The Jack Morgan Songster* (Raleigh, N.C.: Brason & Farrar, 1864), *The Southern Soldiers Prize Songster* (Mobile, Ala.: W. F. Wisely, 1864), and Francis D. Allan, *Allan's Lone Star Ballads* (Galveston, Tex.: J. D. Sawyer, 1874).

27. *Confederate Veteran*, 4 (September 1896), 295; 19 (June 1911), 297.

28. Joseph T. Durkin, ed., *John Dooley Confederate Soldier; His War Journal* (Washington, D.C.: Georgetown University Press, 1945), 54–55, 59.

29. John Esten Cooke, *Wearing of the Gray* (New York: E. B. Treat, 1867), 25, 198–199, 200; William W. Blackford, *War Years with Jeb Stuart* (New York: Scribner's, 1945), 50–51.

30. Alan Lomax, "Folk Song Style," *American Anthropologist*, 61 (December 1959), 929–930. See also Alan Lomax, *The Folk Songs of North America*, passim.

31. Levine, *Black Culture and Black Consciousness*, 5.

32. Professor Edwin Kirkland, for example, collected British ballads in the early 1930s from a wide variety of professionals including fellow faculty members at the University of Tennessee, a bank executive, a physician, and the supervisor of public school music in Knoxville; see Kip Lornell, Notes to *The Kirkland Recordings* (Tennessee Folklore Society TFS–106). Such data, of course, only tells what happened to the ballads; it does not explain the process by which they circulated, nor does it tell us anything about the social or class origins of the professionals who sang the songs. For a perspective that stresses the multiclass possession of the ballads, see John Powell, "In the Lowlands Low," *Southern Folklore Quarterly*, 1 (March 1937), 1–12; and Powell, "Virginia Finds Her Folk Music," in Hazel Gertrude Kinscella, *Music on the Air* (Garden City, N.Y.: Garden City Publishing Co., 1934), 173–174.

33. Alan Lomax, *The Folk Songs of North America*, 169.

34. Emma Bell Miles, *The Spirit of the Mountains* (Knoxville: University of Tennessee Press, 1975; orig. pub., 1905), 68–69.

35. Campbell and Sharp, *English Folk Songs from the Southern Appalachians*, xi.

36. Alan Lomax, *The Folk Songs of North America*, 169.

37. Originally published in *Harper's Magazine*, but also included in Miles, *The Spirit of the Mountains*, 146–171.

38. Alan Lomax, *The Folk Songs of North America*, xix–xx, xxix, 153; see also Cohen, notes to *Going Down the Valley* (New World Records NW 236).

39. Howard W. Odum, *An American Epoch; Southern Portraiture in the National Picture* (New York: Holt, 1930), 180.

40. The statement about Rowland Hill was made by Sam Hinton,

"Folk Songs of Faith," *Sing Out*, 16 (February-March, 1966), 37. For discussions of the folk spirituals, and the contexts in which they developed, see Rhys Isaac, *The Transformation of Virginia, 1740–1790* (Chapel Hill: University of North Carolina Press, 1982); Bruce, *And They All Sang Hallelujah*; Charles Johnson, *The Frontier Camp Meeting* (Dallas: Southern Methodist University Press, 1955); and Richard H. Hulan, "Camp-Meeting Spiritual Folksongs: Legacy of the 'Great Revival in the West,'" Ph.D. dissertation, University of Texas at Austin, 1978.

41. Hulan, "Camp-Meeting Spiritual Folksongs," xxv, 31, 47–49, 91, 93.

42. Hulan, "Camp-Meeting Spiritual Folksongs," 31; Jackson, *White Spirituals*, 31–34; Timothy Alan Smith, "The Southern Folk-Hymn, 1802–1860: A History and Musical Analysis, with Notes on Performance Practice," M.M. thesis, California State University, Fullerton, 1981, p. 52.

43. George Pullen Jackson was the pioneer scholar of the southern shape-note tradition, but see also Eskew, "Shape-Note Hymnody in the Shenandoah Valley, 1816–1860"; Buell E. Cobb, *The Sacred Harp and Its Music* (Athens: University of Georgia Press, 1978); Grace I. Showalter, *The Music Books of Ruebush and Kieffer, 1866–1942* (Richmond: Virginia State Library, 1975); Joel Francis Reed, "Anthony J. Showalter (1858–1924): Southern Educator, Publisher, Composer," Ed.D. dissertation, New Orleans Baptist Theological Seminary, 1975; and Arthur L. Stevenson, *The Story of Southern Hymnology* (Roanoke, Va.: Stone Printing & Manufacturing Co., 1931), 74–76.

44. Gospel music remains one of the most poorly documented forms of American music. Don Cusic, however, has made a useful beginning in *The Sound of Light: A History of Gospel Music* (Bowling Green, Ohio: Bowling Green State University Popular Press, 1990). For the revival roots of gospel music, see James F. Findley, Jr., *Dwight L. Moody, American Evangelist, 1837–1899* (Chicago: University of Chicago Press, 1969), 176–177, 210, 215–216; William McLoughlin, Jr., *Modern Revivalism* (New York: Ronald Press, 1959), 234; and James Downey, "The Music of American Revivalism," Ph.D. dissertation, Tulane University, 1968.

45. Jo Fleming, "James D. Vaughan, Music Publisher," S.M.D. dissertation, Union Theological Seminary, 1972; Reed, "Anthony J. Showalter"; Ottis Knippers, *Who's Who Among Southern Singers and Composers* (Lawrenceburg, Tenn.: J. D. Vaughan, 1937).

46. The first quote comes from Joseph E. Campbell, *The Pentecostal Holiness Church, 1898–1948* (Franklin Springs, Ga.: Publishing House of the Pentecostal Holiness Church, 1951), 235; Parham's quote is found in Sarah E. Parham, *The Life of Charles F. Parham: Founder of the Apostolic Faith Movement* (New York: Garland, 1985; orig. pub., 1930), 117.

47. Josephine M. Washburn, *History and Reminiscences of the Holiness Church Work in Southern California and Arizona* (New York: Garland, 1985; orig. pub., 1912), 87–89, 138, 265. The best historical survey of the Pentecostal movement is Robert Mapes Anderson, *Vision of the Disinherited: The Making of American Pentecostalism* (New York: Oxford University Press, 1979).

48. Hunter Dickinson Farish, ed., *Journal and Letters of Philip Vickers Fithian, 1773–1774: A Plantation Tutor of the Old Dominion* (Williamsburg, Va.: Colonial Williamsburg, 1943), 232.

49. Augustus Baldwin Longstreet, *Georgia Scenes*, second ed. (New York: Harper & Brothers, 1859; orig. pub., 1835), 15.

50. Observations of dances were also clouded by the tendencies to use indiscriminate terminology, or duplicative labels, to describe dances. Charles Read Baskervill, in fact, points out that such imprecision had been common earlier in Great Britain. "Jig," for example, had been used as a generic term for popular song with dance. See Baskervill, *The Elizabethan Jig* (Chicago: University of Chicago Press, 1929), 12–13, 16.

51. Frederick Law Olmsted, *A Journey Through Texas; or, a Saddle-Trip on the Southwestern Frontier* (New York: Mason Brothers, 1861), 384.

52. Charles Lanman, *Adventures in the Wilds of the United States and British American Provinces*, vol. 1 (Philadelphia: John W. Moore, 1856), 441; Frederick Gerstaecker, *Wild Sports of the Far West* (London: Routledge, 1856), 174.

53. Julian Ralph, *Dixie, or Southern Scenes and Sketches* (New York: Harper & Brothers, 1896), 336.

54. Gerstaecker, *Wild Sports of the Far West*, 176; *Spirit of the Times* (September 2, 1843), 30, quoted in George Washington Harris, *High Times and Hard Times*, ed. by Thomas Inge (Nashville: Vanderbilt University Press, 1967).

55. Earl V. Spielman, "Traditional North American Fiddling: A Methodology for the Historical and Comparative Analytical Style Study of Instrumental Musical Traditions," Ph.D. dissertation, University of Wisconsin, 1975, 191.

56. William F. Pope, *Early Days in Arkansas* (Little Rock, Ark.: Frederick W. Allsopp, 1893), 68.

57. Michael Orgill, *Anchored in Love: The Carter Family Story* (Old Tappan, N.J.: Fleming H. Revell Co., 1975), 44–45.

58. Joseph C. Gould, *Old Times in Tennessee* (Nashville: Tavel, Eastman & Howell, 1878), 326.

59. "From the Archives: 'The Arkansas Traveler,'" *JEMF Quarterly*, 6, pt. 2 (Summer 1970), 51–57 (contains a reprint of a *Century* magazine article from March 1896 and suggestions for further research). Cohen, ed., *Minstrels and Tunesmiths*, includes a 1909 recording of the song by Len Spencer and Charles D'Almaine and a lengthy annotation by Cohen, Notes, 10–12.

60. Frank Owsley, *Plain Folk of the Old South* (Baton Rouge: Louisiana State University Press, 1982; orig. pub., 1949).

61. See C. Vann Woodward, *Tom Watson: Agrarian Rebel* (New York: Macmillan, 1938), 101–102, 105; Daniel Merritt Robison, *Bob Taylor and the Agrarian Revolt in Tennessee* (Chapel Hill: University of North Carolina Press, 1935), 40, 44, 63–64; and Paul D. Augsburg, *Bob and Alf Taylor: Their Lives and Lectures* (Morristown, Tenn.: Morristown Book Co., 1925), 42–44, 50–60.

62. Gene Wiggins, "Popular Music and the Fiddler," *JEMF Quarterly*, 15 (Fall 1979), 144–152.

63. Some academic histories, however, do provide many instructive suggestions that will be helpful to future researchers. See Linda Carol Burman Hall, "Southern American Folk Fiddling: Context and Style,"

Ph.D. dissertation, Princeton University, 1974; Hall, "Southern American Folk Fiddle Styles," *Ethnomusicology*, 19 (January 1975), 47–65; Spielman, "Traditional North American Fiddling"; E. Van Der Straeten, *The Romance of the Fiddle* (London: Rebman, 1911); and David D. Boyden, *The History of Violin Playing from Its Origins to 1761* (London: Oxford University Press, 1965). See also the various issues of *Devil's Box*, a journal devoted to old-time fiddling published quarterly by the Tennessee Valley Old Time Fiddlers' Association in Madison, Alabama.

64. Fiddlin' John Carson, *The Old Hen Cackled and the Rooster's Going to Crow* (Rounder 1003); Don Roberson, "Uncle Bunt Stephens: Champion Fiddler," *Old Time Music*, no. 5 (Summer 1972), 4–6.

65. Tommy Jarrell, *Sail Away Ladies*, (County 756), notes by Barry Poss. See also Nancy Dols Neithammer, "Tommy Jarrell's Family Stories, 1830–1925," *The Old-Time Herald*, 3, no. 1 (1991), 22–29.

66. Richard Nevins, notes to *Old-Time Fiddle Classics*, vol. 2, 1927–1934 (County 527).

67. *Fiddling Doc Roberts* (County 412).

68. The American people's fascination with the lore and music of the railroads is well documented in Norm Cohen, *Long Steel Rail: The Railroad in American Folksong* (Urbana: University of Illinois Press, 1981). See also Katie Letcher Lyle, *Scalded to Death By the Steam* (Chapel Hill, N.C.: Algonquin, 1983), and the important anthology of railroad songs on commercial records, *The Railroad in Folksong* (RCA Victor LPV–532), notes by Archie Green.

69. Excellent accounts of the economic transformations in the postwar South include Thomas D. Clark, *The Southern Country Store* (New York: Bobbs-Merrill, 1944); Steven Hahn, *The Roots of Populism: Yeoman Farmers and the Transformation of the Georgia Upcountry, 1850–1890* (New York: Oxford University Press, 1983); Lawrence Goodwyn, *Democratic Promise: The Populist Moment* (New York: Oxford University Press, 1976); Ronald D. Eller, *Miners, Mill Hands, and Mountaineers: The Modernization of the Appalachian South, 1880–1930* (Knoxville: University of Tennessee Press, 1982); and Archie Green, *Only a Miner: Studies in*

Recorded Coal-Mining Songs (Urbana: University of Illinois Press, 1972).
70. See Eller, *Miners, Mill Hands, and Mountaineers*; John Hevener,
Which Side Are You On?: The Harlan County Coal Miners, 1931–1939
(Urbana: University of Illinois Press, 1979); and David Whisnant, *All
That Is Native and Fine: The Politics of Culture in an American Region*
(Chapel Hill: University of North Carolina Press, 1983).

Two. Popular Culture and
the Music of the South

1. Despite the abundance of pop-derived material in the repertories
of folk singers, little scholarship has been devoted to this subject. Norm
Cohen, however, has long been engaged in research that may some-
day result in a major publication devoted to the links between Tin Pan
Alley and folk/country music. His initial findings are found in Norm
Cohen, "Tin Pan Alley's Contribution to Folk Music," *Western Folklore*,
29, no. 1 (1970), 9–20; Norm and Anne Cohen, "Tune Evolution as
an Indicator of Traditional Musical Norms," *Journal of American Folk-
lore*, 86 (January-March 1973), 37–47; Norm Cohen, ed., notes to
Minstrels and Tunesmiths: The Commercial Roots of Early Country Music
(JEMF recording 109); and Norm Cohen, "America's Music: Written
and Recorded," *JEMF Quarterly*, 16 (Fall 1980), 121–131. See also Gene
Wiggins, "Popular Music and the Fiddler," *JEMF Quarterly*, 15, no. 55
(Fall 1979), 144–52; and William C. Ellis, "The Sentimental Mother
Song in American Country Music, 1923–1945," Ph.D. dissertation,
Ohio State University, 1978.

2. James Ward Lee, "The Penny Dreadful as a Folksong," in Wilson M. Hudson and Allen Maxwell, eds., *The Sunny Slopes of Long Ago*
(Dallas: Southern Methodist University Press, 1966), 164.

3. Francis James Child, *The English and Scottish Popular Ballads*, 5 vols.
(Boston: Houghton, Mifflin, 1882–1898).

4. Leslie Shepard, *The Broadside Ballad: A Study in Origin and Meaning* (London: Herbert Jenkins, 1962); Claude M. Simpson, *The British
Broadside Ballad and Its Music* (New Brunswick, N.J.: Rutgers Univer-

sity Press, 1966); G. Malcolm Laws, Jr., *American Balladry from British Broadsides* (Philadelphia: American Folklore Society, 1957).

5. Howard Brockway, "The Quest of the 'Lonesome Tunes,'" in Hazel G. Kinscella, *Music on the Air* (Garden City, N.Y.: Garden City Publishing Co., 1934), 163.

6. Information on the hornpipe and the itinerant entertainers who circulated it can be found in William Chappell, *Popular Music of the Olden Time*, vol. 1 (London: Cramer, Beale & Chappell, 1855); Vuillier Gaston, *A History of Dancing* (New York: Appleton, 1898); and Charles Baskervill, *The Elizabethan Jig* (Chicago: The University of Chicago Press, 1929).

7. Jean Ritchie, *Singing Family of the Cumberlands* (New York: Geordie Music Publishing, 1980; orig. pub., 1955), 73–74.

8. Oscar T. Sonneck, *Early Concert Life in America* (Leipzig, 1907); Julian Mates, *The American Musical Stage before 1800* (New Brunswick, N.J.: Rutgers University Press, 1962); Marian Hannah Winter, "American Theatrical Dancing from 1750 to 1800," *Musical Quarterly*, 24 (January 1938), 58–73.

9. Alan S. Downer, ed., *The Memoir of John Durang* (Pittsburgh: University of Pittsburgh Press, 1966), 22, 43, 69; George L. Chindahl, *A History of the Circus in America* (Caldwell, Idaho: Caxton Printers, 1959), 7–10; Mates, *The American Musical Stage before 1800*, 21–22, 25–26, 129–130, 166.

10. Brooks McNamara, *Step Right Up: An Illustrated History of the Medicine Show* (Garden City, N.Y.: Doubleday, 1976); *Billboard*, 13 (June 2, 1900), 3; *Etude*, 59 (August 1941), 512–513, 566.

11. Lewis Leary, *The Book-Peddling Parson* (Chapel Hill: Algonquin, 1984), 121, 148–149.

12. Isaac Greenwood, *The Circus: Its Origin and Growth prior to 1835* (New York: Dunlap Society, 1898); Maria Ward Brown, *The Life of Dan Rice* (Long Branch, N.J.: Published by the author, 1901); Edward LeRoy Rice, *Monarchs of Minstrelsy, from Daddy Rice to Date* (New York: Kenny Publishing Co., 1911); F. P. Pitzer, "Gay Carusos of the Circus," *Etude*, 60 (October 1942), 676, 707; Esse Forrester O'Brien, *Circus, Cinders to*

Sawdust (San Antonio: Naylor Co., 1959); Chindahl, *A History of the Circus in America*. I examined many of the Clown Songsters in the Harris Collection, Hay Library, Brown University. They included *Nat Austin Comic Song Book* (Boston: J. E. Farwell, 1863); *Billy Andrews Comic Songster* (New York: S. Booth, 1873); *Tom Vance's Circus Songster* (New York: T. W. Strong, 1855); *Jim Ward, the Clown's Comic and Sentimental Songster* (Philadelphia: B. F. Simpson, 1861); *Dan Rice's Great American Song Book* (N.p., 1862); and *Songs Sung by Ben Maginley and Jim Wambold* (Buffalo, N.Y.: Warren, Johnson, n.d.).

13. Phillip Graham, *Show Boats: The History of an American Institution* (Austin: University of Texas Press, 1951); Chindahl, *A History of the Circus in America*, 20–22, 55–56; Robert B. Winans, "The Folk, the Stage, and the Five-String Banjo in the Nineteenth Century," *Journal of American Folklore*, 89 (October-December 1976), 407–437; William Lynwood Montell, *Don't Go Up Kettle Creek: Verbal Legacy of the Upper Cumberland* (Knoxville: University of Tennessee Press, 1983). Montell does not discuss music, but he shows how the Cumberland backcountry was opened up to outside commercial penetration, first by peddlers and later by steamboats (see pp. 37, 128–161).

14. Solomon F. Smith, *Theatrical Management in the West and South for Thirty Years* (New York: Harper & Brothers, 1868); Noah M. Ludlow, *Dramatic Life as I Found It* (New York: B. Bloom, 1966; orig. pub., 1880); John William Ward, *Andrew Jackson: Symbol for an Age* (New York: Oxford University Press, 1955). The information on Shakespeare in Tazewell, Alabama, is from Lawrence Levine, *High Brow, Low Brow: The Emergence of Cultural Hierarchy in America* (Cambridge, Mass.: Harvard University Press, 1988), 20.

15. Carl Wittke, *Tambo and Bones* (Durham, N.C.: Duke University Press, 1930); Robert C. Toll, *Blacking Up: The Minstrel Show in Nineteenth Century America* (New York: Oxford University Press, 1974); Hans Nathan, *Dan Emmett and the Rise of Early Negro Minstrelsy* (Norman: University of Oklahoma Press, 1962); Rice, *Monarchs of Minstrelsy*. For a survey of recorded minstrel humor, see Robert Cogswell, "A Discog-

raphy of Blackface Comedy Dialogs," *JEMF Quarterly*, 15 (Fall 1979), 166–179.

16. Joseph Wynne, "WSM Signs New Comedy Team," *Mountain Broadcast and Prairie Recorder*, 1 (December 1938), 19; George D. Hay, *A Story of the Grand Ole Opry* (Nashville, Tenn.: George D. Hay, 1953), 5, 17, 19.

17. William W. Austin, *"Susannah, Jeanie, and the Old Folks at Home"; The Songs of Stephen C. Foster from His Time to Ours* (New York: Macmillan, 1975), 123, 131–135.

18. Nathan, *Dan Emmett*, 158, 159.

19. For examples of minstrel entertainment found on early recordings, see Cohen, ed., *Minstrels and Tunesmiths*.

20. Nathan, *Dan Emmett*, 126, 128.

21. Letter from Uncle Dave Macon to George D. Hay (May 25, 1933), reprinted in *JEMF Quarterly*, 5, pt. 3 (Autumn 1969), 92–95. "Rock About My Saro Jane" and other representative selections in Macon's repertory can be heard in *The Recordings of Uncle Dave Macon* (County 521).

22. My knowledge of Polk Miller came from *Confederate Veteran*, 3 (January 1895), 7; 3 (June 1895), 194; 6 (April 1898), 160; 8 (June 1900), 288; 21 (December 1913), 598. See also Doug Seroff, "Polk Miller and the Old South Quartette," *JEMF Quarterly*, 18 (Fall-Winter 1982), 147–150, and Seroff, "Polk Miller and the Old South Quartette," *78 Quarterly*, 1, no. 3 (1988), 27–41.

23. Robert B. Winans, "The Folk, the Stage, and the Five-String Banjo in the Nineteenth Century." See also the recorded selections by Van Eps and Ossman in Cohen, ed., *Minstrels and Tunesmiths*.

24. Winans, "The Folk, the Stage, and the Five-String Banjo," 407–437; Winans, "Early Minstrel Show Music," in Glenn Loney, ed., *Musical Theatre in America* (Westport, Conn.: Greenwood Press, 1981), 73, 77, 78. Examples of instruction books used by Winans were *Phil Rice's Correct Method for the Banjo Instructor* (Boston: Oliver Ditson, 1858) and Thomas F. Briggs, *Briggs Banjo Instructor* (Boston: Oliver Ditson, 1855).

William Tallmadge, "The Folk Banjo and Clawhammer Performance Practice in the Upper South: A Study of Origins," in Barry M. Buxton, ed., *The Appalachian Experience: Proceedings of the Sixth Annual Studies Conference* (Boone, N.C.: Appalachian Consortium Press, 1983). Tallmadge also speculates that white people might have learned banjo styles from blacks during the Colonial era, *before* either group moved into the Appalachians.

25. Charles Hamm, *Yesterdays: Popular Song in America* (New York: Norton, 1979), 133–136.

26. Hazel Meyer, *The Gold in Tin Pan Alley* (Philadelphia & New York: Lippincott, 1958); Isaac Goldberg, *Tin Pan Alley* (New York: Day, 1930); Nicholas E. Tawa, *The Way to Tin Pan Alley* (New York: Schirmer Books, 1990); Maxwell Marcuse, *Tin Pan Alley in Gaslight* (Watkins Glen, N.Y.: Century House, 1959).

27. Leonard Levy, *Grace Notes in American History: Popular Sheet Music from 1820 to 1900* (Norman: University of Oklahoma Press, 1967); Levy, *Picture the Song: Lithographs from the Sheet Music of Nineteenth-Century America* (Baltimore & London: Johns Hopkins University Press, 1976). For discussions of the piano's role in nineteenth-century middle-class America see Arthur Loesser, *Men, Women and Pianos* (New York: Simon & Schuster, 1954).

28. Nicholas E. Tawa, "The Ways of Love in the Mid-Nineteenth-Century American Song," *Journal of Popular Culture*, 10 (Fall 1976), 340.

29. No single or readily available source of Tin Pan Alley items that became folk songs exists for the modern student. Sigmund Spaeth, though, compiled two lighthearted studies of many of the sentimental songs: *Read 'Em and Weep: The Songs You Forgot to Remember* (Garden City, N.Y.: Doubleday, Page, 1926); and *Weep Some More My Lady* (Garden City, N.Y.: Doubleday, Page, 1927).

30. Edward B. Marks, a successful writer and publisher on Tin Pan Alley, left a delightful memoir of his days in the songwriting business: Marks, as told to Abbott J. Liebling, *They All Sang: From Tony Pastor to Rudy Vallee* (New York: Viking, 1935), esp. 18, 33, 44.

31. Austin, *"Susannah, Jeanie, and the Old Folks at Home,"* 132.

32. In his autobiography, *After the Ball*, Charles K. Harris told of a chance meeting with Booker T. Washington on a train in 1909. After Washington asked how he could write such "delightful southern melodies" without ever visiting the South, Harris replied that it was "all imagination. I had to inquire if there was corn raised in Virginia and if there were hills in Carolina. This information was given me by my office superintendent, Mr. Blaise, a native Southerner, and my imagination did the rest." Harris, *After the Ball: Forty Years of Melody* (New York: Frank-Maurice, 1926), 318.

33. The altering of professionally composed popular songs, and their transmogrification into folk or hillbilly songs, was not simply a consequence of imperfect "folk" transmission. Hillbilly musicians and songwriters sometimes consciously changed melodies and lyrics in dramatic ways. For example, Charles K. Harris's "Ma Filipino Babe," about a black American sailor's experiences, acquired a new melody and a new racial identity for its sailor protagonist by the time it appeared on a commercial hillbilly recording in 1937 as "Filipino Baby." Compare the original song, in Charles K. Harris, *Popular Songster* (Milwaukee: Harris, 1899), with the recordings made by Billy Cox in 1937 and Lloyd "Cowboy" Copas in 1944 (King 505). Cox claimed to have written the song under the inspiration of letters written by his uncle, who had married a girl while serving military duty in the Philippines. See Ken Davidson, notes to Billy Cox, *The Dixie Song Bird* (Kanawha 305). Similarly, Harris's "All For the Love of a Girl" preserved only its title and a few key lines after Johnny Horton released his recorded version in the late 1950s. See *Charles K. Harris Complete Songster* (Chicago: Frederick J. Drake, 1903). For a discussion of the problems surrounding the metamorphoses of popular songs into folk songs, see Cohen and Cohen, "Tune Evolution as an Indicator of Traditional Musical Norms," esp. 41–42.

34. No published biography of Hays exists. The life and career presented here have been reconstructed from materials found in the following repositories: The Filson Club in Louisville, Kentucky; the Manuscripts Section in the Kentucky Library at Western Kentucky University

in Bowling Green; materials in the possession of Hays's niece, Mrs. Clark Kaye, in Louisville; and an M.A. thesis by Martha Carol Chrisman, "Will S. Hays: a Biography," University of Minnesota, 1980. I am particularly indebted to Mrs. Kaye for her generous assistance.

35. *The Modern Meetin' House and Other Poems* (Louisville: Courier-Journal, 1874); *Songs and Poems* (Louisville: Courier-Journal, 1886); *Poems and Songs* (Louisville: C. T. Dearing, 1895).

36. There is no collection of Hays's songs either in print or on recordings. I have looked at copies in the Music Division of the Library of Congress, at the Kentucky Library at Western Kentucky University in Bowling Green, and at the Filson Club in Louisville.

37. Meyer, *The Gold in Tin Pan Alley*, 27; Hamm, *Yesterdays*, 265.

38. Carl Sandburg, *The American Songbag* (New York: Harcourt, Brace, 1927), 89, 259.

39. *Southland Spirituals* (Chicago: Rodeheaver, 1936), no. 31.

40. Alma Gluck's 1913 recording is on Victor 64809. Another recording of the song, along with commentary about its recorded history, is in Cohen, ed., *Minstrels and Tunesmiths*. Fiddlin' John's recording, Okeh 4890, is anthologized on Rounder 1003. For a discussion of the role played by Carson and the song in early country music, see Gene Wiggins, *Fiddlin' Georgia Crazy: Fiddlin' John Carson, His Real World, and the World of His Songs* (Urbana: University of Illinois Press, 1987), 221–225.

41. Advertisements for "Molly Darling" in successive issues of *Stand By* (a journal published by WLS in Chicago) noted that the song could be purchased as sheet music from the Music Library at WLS: Vol. 2, nos. 40, 41, 42 (November 14, 21, 28, 1936). Lair called its melody "the sweetest ever written by that grand old folk song writer, Will S. Hays." Vol. 2, no. 41, 13.

42. Whitstein Brothers, *Old Time Duets* (Rounder 0264); Blue Sky Boys (Bluebird B–8482).

43. Eddy Arnold, "Molly Darling" (RCA 20–2489). Arnold said that he found the song "in an old folio and it was written in the old-fashioned way. I started changing it around so it would fit the Eddy Arnold style": Eddy Arnold, notes to *Legendary Performances* (RCA CPL 2–4885).

44. Flatt and Scruggs, "Jimmie Brown, the Newsboy" (Columbia 20830), and in *Foggy Mountain Jamboree* (Columbia CL 1019). The Carter Family recorded their version of the song on November 25, 1929 (Victor V–40255 and Bluebird B–5543).

45. Although "Shamus O'Brien" was written as a romantic love song, it is now played most often as a fiddle tune. The fate of this song, and other "Irish" dialect numbers written by Hays, should be evaluated to determine their histories in the British Isles. Hays was quoted in 1898 as saying that "they are singing my songs in Scotland now. Long ago I wrote a collection of Scotch songs under the name of Allen Percy and they had a great sale." Interview with Will Hays by Dick Work, newspaper clipping (circa 1898), in the possession of Mrs. Clark Kaye, Louisville, Kentucky. An obituary in the *Chicago Inter-Ocean* (also an undated clipping) said that Hays "was next to his best when he assayed the Irish melody. His "Nora O'Neill" and his "Shamus O'Brien" have been incorporated into the ballad collection of the Emerald Isle."

46. The subtitle of Sigmund Spaeth, *Read 'Em and Weep: The Songs You Forgot to Remember*.

Three. Mountaineers and Cowboys: Country Music's Search for Identity

1. Archie Green, "Hillbilly Music: Source and Symbol," *Journal of American Folklore*, 78 (July-September, 1965), 223.

2. See Bill C. Malone, *Southern Music/American Music* (Lexington: University Press of Kentucky, 1979).

3. Green, "Hillbilly Music," 223.

4. H. L. Mencken, "Sahara of the Bozart," *A Mencken Chrestomathy* (New York: Alfred A. Knopf, Inc., 1920) in Thomas D. Clark, ed., *The South since Reconstruction* (New York & Indianapolis: Bobbs-Merrill, 1973), 551–554.

5. Arthur Smith, "Hillbilly Folk Music," *Etude*, 51 (March 1933), 154, 208.

6. Archie Green has long been interested in the visual representations

of country and folk music. See his "Commercial Music Graphics" series in the *JEMF Quarterly*.

7. John A. Lomax, *Cowboy Songs and Other Frontier Ballads* (New York: Sturgis and Walton, 1910); Cecil Sharp and Olive Dame Campbell, *English Folk Songs from the Southern Appalachians* (New York: Putnam's, 1917). For a discussion of other early folk song collections that contained southern material, see D. K. Wilgus, *Anglo-American Folksong Scholarship since 1898* (New Brunswick, N.J.: Rutgers University Press, 1959).

8. Bill C. Malone, *Country Music, USA* (Austin: University of Texas Press, rev. ed., 1985), 35–36. Michael Lee Masterson, "Sounds of the Frontier: Music in Buffalo Bill's Wild West," Ph.D. dissertation, University of New Mexico, 1990. Masterson demonstrates that the songs heard in these shows came from popular music, and not from the western folk tradition. Nevertheless, the cowboys seen in the shows would have reaffirmed the concept of the Show Business Cowboy.

9. Campbell and Sharp, *English Folk Songs from the Southern Appalachians*, viii.

10. The best discussion of Carson's life and career is Gene Wiggins, *Fiddlin' Georgia Crazy; Fiddlin' John Carson, His Real World, and the World of His Songs* (Urbana: University of Illinois Press, 1987).

11. The best discussion of the role played by local-color literature in building a romantic conception of the southern mountains is Herbert D. Shapiro, *Appalachia On Our Mind: The Southern Mountains and Mountaineers in the American Consciousness, 1870–1920* (Chapel Hill: University of North Carolina Press, 1978).

12. Joseph Wilson, notes to Al Hopkins, *The Hillbillies* (County 405).

13. Edwin T. Arnold, "Al, Abner, and Appalachia," *Appalachian Journal*, 17 (Spring 1990), 266.

14. *Billboard*, 41 (May 11, 1929), 14, 15, 25, listed three groups—the Hillbillies, the Blue Ridge Ramblers, and the Virginia Mountaineers—as current vaudeville attractions in New York City.

15. Lunsford has been discussed in the following publications: Loyal Jones, *Minstrel of the Appalachians: The Story of Bascom Lamar Luns-*

ford (Boone, N.C.: Appalachian Consortium Press, 1984); Loyal Jones, "The Minstrel of the Appalachians: Bascom Lamar Lunsford at 91," *JEMF Quarterly*, 9, pt. 1 (Spring 1973), 2–7; David E. Whisnant, "Finding the Way Between the Old and the New: The Mountain Dance and Folk Festival and Bascom Lamar Lunsford's Work as a Citizen," *Appalachian Journal*, 7 (Autumn-Winter, 1979–80), 135–154; and Bascom Lamar Lunsford, "Annual Mountain Dance and Folk Festival," *Disc Collector*, no. 18 (circa 1962), 3–6.

16. For information on Buell Kazee, see Charles G. Bowen, "Buell Kazee: The Genuine Article," *Sing Out*, 20 (September-October 1970), 13–17, 58; "Buell Kazee Talking," *Old Time Music*, no. 6 (Autumn 1972), 6–10; Tony Russell, "Buell Kazee, 1900–76," *Old Time Music*, no. 21 (Summer 1976), 17–18; and Buell Kazee and Gene Bluestein, notes to *Buell Kazee Sings and Plays* (Folkways FS 3810).

17. Journalist Frank Tannenbaum contributed to the public perception of southern iniquity with his *Darker Phases of the South* (London: Putnam's, 1924). For historical perspective, consult George Tindall, "The Benighted South: Origins of a Modern Image," *Virginia Quarterly Review*, 40 (Spring 1964), 281–294.

18. Discussions of the Carter Family include Ed Kahn, "The Carter Family: A Reflection of Changes in Society," Ph.D. dissertation, University of California, Los Angeles, 1970; Archie Green, Norm Cohen, and William H. Koon, notes to *The Carter Family on Border Radio* (JEMF 101); Archie Green, "The Carter Family's 'Coal Miner's Blues,'" *Southern Folklore Quarterly*, 25 (December 1961), 226–237; John Atkins, "The Carter Family," in Bill C. Malone and Judith McCulloh, eds., *Stars of Country Music* (Urbana: University of Illinois Press, 1976), 95–120; and John Atkins, Bob Coltman, Alec Davidson, and Kip Lornell, *The Carter Family* (London: Old Time Music, 1973). The last work includes a valuable discography.

19. The two best biographical sketches of Kincaid are D. K. Wilgus, "Bradley Kincaid," in *Stars of Country Music*, 86–94; and Loyal Jones, *Radio's "Kentucky Mountain Boy": Bradley Kincaid* (Berea, Ky.: Appalachian Center, 1980).

20. The "hillybilly" reference appeared in Bradley Kincaid, *Favorite Old-Time Songs and Mountain Ballads* (Chicago: WLS, 1930), while the comment about "Anglo-Saxon" origins appeared in his first songbook, *My Favorite Mountain Ballads and Old-Time Songs* (Chicago: WLS, 1928). In a letter to H. E. Taylor of Berea College, November 24, 1932, Kincaid wrote, "These hillbillies sing through their noses, and most of their numbers are bum songs or jail songs" (Berea Archives, Berea College, Kentucky).

21. Jones, *Radio's "Kentucky Mountain Boy,"* 2, 28 (Archie Green's quote comes from the introduction, 2).

22. Ibid., 8.

23. This first generation of urban or concert performers of folk songs has not yet received adequate biographical or interpretive treatment. Their stories remain buried, for the most part, in such "high-art" music journals as *Etude* and *Musical Courier*.

24. *Cincinnati Enquirer* (September 18, 1938).

25. Jean Ritchie, *Singing Family of the Cumberlands* (New York: Geordie Music Publishing, 1980; orig. pub. 1955, Oak Publications).

26. D. K. Wilgus, *Anglo-American Folksong Scholarship since 1898* (New Brunswick, N.J.: Rutgers University Press, 1959), 209; Wilgus, notes to *Edna Ritchie* (Folk-Legacy FSA-3); Wilgus, "On the Record," *Kentucky Folklore Record*, 8 (July-September 1962), 111–112.

27. David Whisnant, *All That is Native and Fine* (Chapel Hill: University of North Carolina Press, 1983), 93–97 passim; Virginia Anne Chambers, "Music in Four Kentucky Mountain Settlement Schools," Ph.D. dissertation, University of Michigan, 1970.

28. Jean Ritchie, notes to *Precious Memories* (Folkways FA 2427).

29. Ritchie, *Singing Family of the Cumberlands*, 73–76.

30. Ritchie has been far from blind to these transforming forces, and has in fact written some fine songs of social commentary and protest, including "Black Waters" and "The L&N Don't Stop Here Anymore."

31. Bentley Ball's version of "The Dying Cowboy" can be heard on Cohen, ed., *Minstrels and Tunesmiths*; several of the recorded cowboy singers of the 1920s appear on the anthology *Authentic Cowboys and*

their Western Folksongs (RCA Victor Vintage LPV-522), notes by Fred Hoeptner. John White compiled a selection of his cowboy articles under the title *Git Along, Little Dogies: Songs and Songmakers of the American West* (Urbana: University of Illinois Press, 1975).

32. Nolan Porterfield, *Jimmie Rodgers: The Life and Times of America's Blue Yodeler* (Urbana: University of Illinois Press, 1979). See also Malone, *Country Music, USA*, 89–90, 141–142.

33. Evidence of the radio cowboy's omnipresence can easily be found in newspaper radio logs and hillbilly magazines and songbooks from the 1930s and 1940s. For examples, look at the various issues of *Mountain Broadcast and Prairie Recorder* and *Broadcasting and Broadcast Advertising.* "Green Grow the Lilacs" influence is discussed in Stanley Green, "'Oklahoma!': Its Origin and Influence," *American Music*, 2 (Winter 1984), 88–94.

34. Gene Autry, with Mickey Herskowitz, *Back in the Saddle Again* (Garden City, N.Y.: Doubleday, 1978); Douglas B. Green, "Gene Autry," in *Stars of Country Music*, 142–156.

35. Green, "Gene Autry," 154. See also Green, "The Singing Cowboy: An American Dream," *Journal of Country Music*, 7 (May 1978), 4–61. Other useful discussions of both mythic and real cowboys, and their performance of music, include John G. Cawelti, "Cowboys, Indians, Outlaws," *American West*, 1 (Spring 1964), 29–35, 77–79; Sam D. Ratcliffe, "The American Cowboy: A Note on the Development of a Musical Image," *JEMF Quarterly*, 20 (Spring-Summer 1984), 2–7; Thomas S. Johnson, "That Ain't Country: The Distinctiveness of Commercial Western Music," *JEMF Quarterly*, 17 (Summer 1981), 75–84; and Bob Bovee, "Way Out West: Cowboy Songs and Singers," *Old-Time Herald*, 2 (August-October 1989), 6–9, 43.

36. Interviews with Milly Good McCluskey, by telephone from Cincinnati, Ohio, August 11, 1973, and in Cincinnati, July 16, 1990. A good representation of the sisters' style and songs is *The Girls of the Golden West* (Sonyatone STR202).

37. Ken Griffis has done the best work on the Sons of the Pioneers: *Hear My Song: The Story of the Celebrated Sons of the Pioneers* (Los

Angeles: John Edwards Memorial Foundation, 1974). He also edited and wrote the notes for *The Sons of the Pioneers* (JEMF 102). The Farr Brothers can be heard performing instrumentals on *The Farr Brothers: Texas Crapshooter* (JEMF 107).

38. The best discussion of the mythic lure of the West remains Henry Nash Smith, *Virgin Land: The American West as Symbol and Myth* (Cambridge, Mass.: Harvard University Press, 1950), esp. 90–111. See also David Dary, *Cowboy Culture: A Saga of Five Centuries* (New York: Avon, 1981), 332–338. For Hank Penny, see Ken Griffis, "Hank Penny: The Original 'Outlaw'?," *JEMF Quarterly*, 17 (Spring-Summer 1982), 5–9.

39. Griffis, "Hank Penny," 6; Charles Townsend, *San Antonio Rose: The Life and Music of Bob Wills* (Urbana: University of Illinois Press, 1976). Very useful musical collections include *The Bob Wills Anthology* (Columbia KG 32416), notes by Bill Ivey; *Okeh Western Swing* (Epic EG37324), notes by John Morthland; and *Milton Brown and His Brownies* (MCA 1509).

40. Malone, *Country Music, USA*, chap. 5, esp. 157–170.

41. The principal biographer of Wills is Charles Townsend, *San Antonio Rose*, and "Bob Wills," in *Stars of Country Music*, 157–178.

42. Guy Logsdon tries to link Western Swing directly to the ranch dances of Texas and Oklahoma in "The Cowboy's Bawdy Music," in Charles W. Harris and Buck Rainey, eds., *The Cowboy: Six-Shooters, Songs, and Sex* (Norman: University of Oklahoma Press, 1976), 136.

43. Townsend, *San Antonio Rose*, 3, 36.

44. Roy Acuff, *Great Speckled Bird and Other Favorites* (Harmony HL 7082).

45. The best discussions of Roy Acuff are Elizabeth Schlappi, "Roy Acuff and His Smoky Mountain Boys Discography," *Disc Collector*, no. 23 (1966), and her essay on Acuff in *Stars of Country Music*, 179–201.

46. "Precious Jewel" (Okeh 05956).

47. Loretta Lynn, with George Vecsey, *Coal Miner's Daughter* (New York: Warner Books, 1976); William Ivey, "Chet Atkins," in *Stars of Country Music*, 274–289.

48. Neil Rosenberg, *Bluegrass: A History* (Urbana: University of Illinois Press, 1985); Mayne Smith, "An Introduction to Bluegrass," *Journal of American Folklore*, 78 (1965), 245–256; Ralph Rinzler, "Bill Monroe," in *Stars of Country Music*, 202–221; Robert Cantwell, *Bluegrass Breakdown: The Making of the Old Southern Sound* (Urbana: University of Illinois Press, 1984).

49. Cantwell, *Bluegrass Breakdown*, 143. See Mayne Smith's excellent review of Cantwell's book in *JEMF Quarterly*, 20 (Spring-Summer 1984), 33–38.

50. Lester Flatt and Earl Scruggs, with Mother Maybelle Carter, *Songs of the Famous Carter Family* (Columbia CL1664).

51. Cantwell, *Bluegrass Breakdown*, 58.

52. See the letters section in *Bluegrass Unlimited*, 26 (August 1991), 26 (December 1991).

53. The folk revival still awaits its historian, but Norm Cohen has made a valuable beginning with his edited and annotated collection of recordings for the Smithsonian Institution: *Folk Song America: A 20th Century Revival* (Smithsonian Collection of Recordings RD 046). One of the prime sources of the revival, the great 3-volume *Anthology of American Folk Music* (Folkways Records FA 2951-FA 2953), is still in print. Joe Klein, *Woody Guthrie* (New York: Knopf, 1980), is an outstanding biography of the godfather of the revival, and a useful survey of the music's 1930s roots.

54. Each of these musicians had been introduced to urban audiences through the *Anthology of American Folk Music*. They can also be heard on the following recordings: *Dock Boggs: Legendary Singer and Banjo Player* (Folkways FA2351), and *Dock Boggs* (Folkways FH 5458), both edited by Mike Seeger; Clarence Ashley, *Old Time Music at Clarence Ashley's*, pt. 1 (Folkways FA 2355), and pt. 2 (Folkways FA 2359), edited by Eugene Earle and Ralph Rinzler; *Buell Kazee Sings and Plays* (Folkways FS 3810), and *Buell Kazee* (June Appal JA 009), with notes and discography by Loyal Jones.

55. Notes to *New Lost City Ramblers* (Folkways FA 2396).

56. John Cohen and Mike Seeger, eds., *New Lost City Ramblers Song-*

book (New York: Oak Publications, 1964). Alice Foster Gerrard has done much to keep the revival flame alive through her outstanding singing, and through the editing of *The Old-Time Herald* (published quarterly in Durham, North Carolina). A good anthology of musicians who have continued to play old-time music in our own day is *The Young Fogies* (Heritage Records 056).

57. The review of Doc Watson, *My Dear Old Southern Home*, was by Rick Swenson, in *The Record Roundup*, no. 78, issue 4 (1991), 29. Cohen, notes to *Minstrels and Tunesmiths*.

58. Charles Faurot produced a series of excellent recordings of Texas fiddle music for County Records: *Texas Farewell, Texas Fiddlers* (County 517), originally recorded between 1922 and 1930; and *Texas Fiddle Favorites* (County 703) and *Texas Hoedown* (County 707), both composed of modern recordings. Eck Robertson can be heard on *Eck Robertson: Master Fiddler* (Sonyatone).

59. Two "tribute" albums are particularly valuable: Ray Price, *San Antonio Rose* (Columbia CL 1756); and Merle Haggard, *A Tribute to the Best Damn Fiddle Player in the World* (Capitol ST 638).

60. One of the best examples of the Bob Wills/Texas mystique is a recording, complete with enthusiastic audience response, by Waylon Jennings, "Bob Wills is Still the King" (RCA APLI–1062).

61. Guy Logsdon has produced and edited a collection of cowboy songs previously recorded for Folkways, which includes such people as Woody Guthrie, Leadbelly, and Harry McClintock: *Cowboys Sing on Folkways* (Smithsonian/Folkways CD SF 40043).

62. Waylon Jennings, *Ladies Love Outlaws* (RCA LSP–4751). Jennings and Nelson, and a few of their friends, recorded still another collection of songs which contributed even further to the hype surrounding the outlaw craze: *Wanted: The Outlaws* (RCA APLI–1321). The best biography of Jennings is R. Serge Denisoff, *Waylon* (Knoxville: University of Tennessee Press, 1983).

63. A substantial body of publications exist for Willie Nelson and the Austin music scene: These include Willie Nelson, with Bud Shrake, *Willie: An Autobiography* (New York: Simon & Schuster, 1988); Jan

Reid, *The Improbable Rise of Redneck Rock* (Austin: Heidelberg Press, 1974); Archie Green, "Austin's Cosmic Cowboys: Words in Collision," in Richard Bauman and Roger D. Abrahams, eds., *And Other Neighborly Names: Social Process and Cultural Image in Texas Folklore* (Austin: University of Texas Press, 1981), 152–194; Green, "Michael Adams: Honky Tonk Paintings," *JEMF Quarterly*, 18 (Fall-Winter 1982), 155–165; Green, "Midnight and Other Cowboys," *JEMF Quarterly*, 11, pt. 3 (Autumn 1975), 137–152; and Nick Spitzer, "Bob Wills is Still the King: Romantic Regionalism and Convergent Culture in Central Texas," *JEMF Quarterly*, 2, pt. 4 (Winter 1975), 191–197.

64. James N. Gregory, *American Exodus: The Dust Bowl Migration and Okie Culture in California* (New York: Oxford University Press, 1989), is an excellent account of the self-affirming role that music played in the lives of the Okie migrants.

65. The Osborne Brothers, "Rocky Top" (Decca 32242); Waylon Jennings (with Willie Nelson), "Luckenbach, Texas (Back to the Basics of Love)," in *Ol' Waylon* (RCA APLI-2317); Merle Haggard, "Big City" (Epic FET 37593).

Index

Abbey, M. E., 63
Acuff, Roy, 99, 100–101, 102
African-American culture:
  interrelationship with white
  folk culture, 15–18, 19, 27, 34,
  39, 52, 71, 73, 97, 107; influ-
  ence on pentecostal music, 32;
  and white banjo styles, 54–55,
  129–30 (n. 24)
"After the Ball," 43, 58
Albion's Seed, 11
Allen, Jules Verne, 89
Allen, Rex, 93
"All for the Love of a Girl," 131
  (n. 33)
"Amarillo by Morning," 113

American Association of
  University Women, 85
American Songbag, The, 63
Anglo-Saxon myth, 2, 10, 45, 73,
  83, 105
Appalachian region, 21, 22, 76,
  82, 84, 90, 99–100, 102, 103,
  104, 105, 106, 108
"Arkansas Traveler, The," 37, 53
Arnold, Eddy, 65, 132 (n. 43)
Asheville, N.C., 89
Ashley, Clarence, 107
Ashlock, Jesse, 109, 112
Asleep at the Wheel, 109
Atchison, Tex, 96
Atkins, Chet, 101